MW00929731

Building
Heaven
on Earth

CLAIMING OUR HUMAN SPIRIT

DWIGHT WEBB, PhD

iUniverse, Inc.
Bloomington

Building Heaven on Earth
Claiming Our Human Spirit

Copyright © 2012 by Dwight Webb, PhD.

All rights reserved. No part of this book may be used or reproduced by any means, graphic, electronic, or mechanical, including photocopying, recording, taping or by any information storage retrieval system without the written permission of the publisher except in the case of brief quotations embodied in critical articles and reviews.

iUniverse books may be ordered through booksellers or by contacting:

iUniverse
1663 Liberty Drive
Bloomington, IN 47403
www.iuniverse.com
1-800-Authors (1-800-288-4677)

Because of the dynamic nature of the Internet, any web addresses or links contained in this book may have changed since publication and may no longer be valid. The views expressed in this work are solely those of the author and do not necessarily reflect the views of the publisher, and the publisher hereby disclaims any responsibility for them.

Any people depicted in stock imagery provided by Thinkstock are models, and such images are being used for illustrative purposes only.
Certain stock imagery © Thinkstock.

ISBN: 978-1-4759-1338-5 (sc)
ISBN: 978-1-4759-1339-2 (hc)
ISBN: 978-1-4759-1337-8 (ebk)

Library of Congress Control Number: 2012906645

Printed in the United States of America

iUniverse rev. date: 05/18/2012

TABLE OF CONTENTS
CHAPTERS AND HEADINGS

FOREWORD

"And the old white horse galloped away in the meadow." This is an interesting image in T. S. Eliot's poem "Journey of the Magi." It was Eliot's metaphor for the hardscrabble spirituality of the ancient scriptures giving way to the spirituality of compassion. Dwight Webb's book, *Building Heaven on Earth: Claiming our Spirit Within*, is an important pivotal point contributing to the kicking off of the next dispensation.

If we are to actualize our full potential, Dr. Webb says we must claim our spiritual core, the source of our everyday actions of love, respect, and kindness. He points out how accepting the fixed answers of various religions has led us away from discovering the vitality of our inner spirituality and accepting the mysteries of the universe and life on our planet.

He makes the case that it is the evolution of our consciousness that clarifies our sense of capabilities and possibilities as we work together to manage the planet's resources. His highly original ideas remind us that it is up to us to see and do our part as co-creators, tapping into the strength of our inner spiritual life. He points out that as our spiritual consciousness evolves, we will discard irrelevant dogmas as new principles for living are agreed upon, and reminds us that we do not need a venerable, eternally bearded male in the heavens to threaten us into loving ways. Webb reminds us that the God of the heavens that we have historically accepted will not deliver on our individual requests, because there is no such God responding to our six billion petitions. Our personal spirituality requires that we take responsibility for our own lives, our own "patch," and our own communities, as we create the spirit of love and cooperation that becomes the abiding path for humanity. This is the natural life force of God that is within all life.

Dr. Webb argues forcefully against those who sow division through prejudice, greed, and polarized cultural conditions that work against the need for global cooperation. It is from our inner human spirit wherein we have the bonds of compassion for each other as human beings that we will build relationships of compassion and respect among our diverse yet interconnected cultures. Because religions are limited to their own culture of believers, our emerging spiritual consciousness must transcend those limitations and work to build a common infrastructure of intercultural trust. This will be the foundation upon which we will *build heaven on earth together.*

—Paul Treacy, PhD

PREFACE

Ode To A Natural God

All life tuned to the rhythms of the Universe
Abundance and beauty everywhere,
In awe, and grateful to be alive,
I am humbled by the mystery of it all

For the last few decades, I have been writing down my ideas about our human spirit, saving these musings by randomly tossing notes into my desk drawer. There they remained, out of sight and mostly out of mind, while I pursued other tangents, busying myself with projects that I thought might fare more favorably in my effort to contribute to my profession. But the fact that I saved these notes on scraps of paper tells me that I must have had some inkling that these ideas were important truths for me. I sensed that I would someday get back to addressing them. It's interesting to me how some aspects of our spirit may lie dormant, subdued by the norms of our current cultural immersion yet resilient enough to say, *Save these ideas for "later."* In the last few years, that "later" has been emerging into "now" as I have gathered my ideas, connecting and integrating them into a more coherent stream of my spiritual development.

It was in 1994 when I first called myself out of my self-imposed spiritual closet and presented my ideas to professionals in a workshop entitled Counseling and Spirituality. The following year, my friend and colleague Liam McCarthy invited me to speak at the inauguration of his Personal Counselling Institute in Dublin, Ireland. He said, "You can speak on anything you want." I told him I had been developing my ideas about human spirituality and would like to talk about them. His enthusiastic acceptance was most encouraging. The title of my paper was *Claiming Our Spirituality: Teachable, Tangible, and Too Long in the Closet.*

A few years later, I began working on my book *The Soul of Counseling*. When I remembered that the word "psychology" *literally means* "the study of the soul." I wanted to challenge my colleagues to also remember and to acknowledge our oversight. I had been in the field of counseling psychology for more than four decades and had never heard the word soul mentioned in any classroom, nor had I seen it on any local, regional, state, national or international programs in counseling. I also never saw the word soul included in any syllabus or textbook in counseling. In short, there had been zero attention given to the questions of our human *soul* in professional counseling until the turning of the twenty first century.

The concept of soul remains too ethereal for the academic and research world of psychology. From the beginning, the discipline of psychology has chosen to be on the safe side of things, keeping their focus on what can be reasonably measured, such as social behavior, cognition, emotion, and the stimulus/response patterns of mice, pigeons, and other animals held in their laboratories. In their attempts to establish their profession as a respected and viable science, they have avoided anything that even hinted at human spirituality. Pastoral psychology is an exception, but their ideas on spirituality are narrowly defined, being paired and bonded with religion.

Soul and human spirituality have not been studied as a separate entity from religion. Religions have claimed that spirituality belongs in their domain, and they sell us on the idea that they will take care of our spiritual lives for us. Yielding to that claim has been a mistake because our personal spiritual lives may not be reduced to fit within the confines of any religion.

Spirituality is the core of our humanness, and religions are but one avenue to this overarching dimension of our lives. Our spiritual lives are the essence of who we are and how we express our vitality—our aliveness—whether we are religious or not. It is our compassion, kindness, and forgiveness that are based in love and respect for all of life. These are the dominant impulses within our human family and are much larger than the scope of religion. When we are free of the doctrines and dogma of most religions, these impulses are less encumbered as we discover our spiritual autonomy.

It is important to understand that our spiritual nature is tangible, observable, and experienced in very real terms in all of our significant relationships. Our soul and spirit are our avenue of connecting with others and are always salient, even in the subtle and nuanced expressions of our tone of voice and our body language. The important exchanges we have with others are essentially expressions of our spiritual energy, and when they are compassionate, we feel the treasure of receiving love, respect, and caring from another.

The central goal of this book is to bring our human spirit into prominent focus in our everyday life experiences. By bringing our spirituality out of the heavens and *down to Earth*, we experience personal authenticity in our relationships. These bonds between people are not burdened by the myths and supernatural beliefs that religions impose.

Redefining Spirituality

Many books deal with love, compassion, and forgiveness, but very few of these claim that it is our spirit within that reveals our authenticity in these acts of grace. It would be a mistake in our multicultural global world, if acceptance, understanding, and other acts of compassion were limited by being framed in terms that are biased by the religions within each culture. Spiritual acts can and will stand alone across national borders, and will stand toe to toe with the stubborn differences between religions. When we recognize that the common ground we share with people of other cultures arises from our *human spirit, and not from our religions, we will transcend the differences that keep us in conflict.*

I was recently in a major bookstore, and noticed the various heading markers along the aisles identifying areas of interest for their customers. In the *Spirituality section* there were remarkably few offerings. What they did have were Tarot cards, Astrology booklets, and a few books on Eastern traditions, such as the *I Ching*. I was puzzled by the fact that there were *no* offerings of a more substantial and comprehensive examination of human spirituality. I found this void to be an astonishing statement about our current lack of multicultural spiritual awareness. Our common human spirituality of mutual respect, trust, and openness is our bridge for transcending individual differences between religions. How else will we find peace among nations?

Our personal spirituality must not be relinquished to religions or any institutions or cults of devotion that offer supernatural explanations.

Likewise, we need to avoid cults and such that offer simplistic techniques, or superstitious rituals as a substitute for expressing our genuine spirituality. *Everything we have passion for comes from the vitality of our spirit.* Claiming our spirituality is about opening to our inner life where we discover our values and choices along with our meaning and purposes.

It is always a choice we have to bring spiritual qualities, such as empathy, compassion, and respect, into our daily lives. We need to remind ourselves that we are not here just to take care of the business of making a living but that we are here to serve our families and communities for the *common good.* Too often we go about our daily activities and neglect to honor or even recognize the spiritual nature of our service to others.

Where is it written that in order to be spiritual, we must belong to a religion? Who sets these rules? Just because I don't choose to go to church (temple, mosque, or some other place of worship), does not mean that I don't have a strong belief about a God as a higher power, a creator, or some other such magnificent and inexplicable force known by any other name. To the contrary, I see the work of a Natural God all around me in the ongoing evolution of life.

For as long as I can remember, I have believed that there must be a God, but I have been quietly suspicious of the gods presented by various religions and their denominations. Churches requiring me to buy into their story line and fool myself into pretending that I believe them, or that I even began to understand them, simply assumed too much. Religion's supernatural stories and rules for believing were too confining, too confusing, and too exclusive for me. I just could not do it.

Most religions require followers to have a faith that can't be questioned. This unspoken pledge of loyalty serves as a cloak behind which devotees may find comfort in not having to answer hard questions, since no questions are allowed. Blind devotion to religious protocol keeps people from going within to seek their personal spiritual awareness. Choosing to hold on to blind devotion is to offer no challenges to existing doctrine. Apple founder Steve Jobs said in his address to the graduates of Stanford University's class of 2005: "Your time is limited, so don't waste it living someone else's life. Don't be trapped by dogma—which is living with the results of other peoples thinking. Don't let the noise of other's opinions drown out your own inner music. And most importantly, have the courage to follow your heart and intuition. They somehow already know what you truly want to become. Everything else is secondary."

This book encourages readers to question any existing doctrine if it does not make sense. For example, ask yourselves about your beliefs on the following questions: Is God is a human figure? Does the God to whom you pray when asking for favors dwell in the heavens? Does your God play favorites? Can you accept that our universe and our own lives on this amazing and magnificent planet we call Earth are a mystery? Can you accept that God is a mystery?

Consider the spiritual source of your own compassion, empathy, respect, forgiveness, faith, hope, generosity, courage, and trustworthiness. Do these not come from the source of your own soul? Are these not examples of the building blocks for expressing and experiencing your spirit? I suggest that all readers ask themselves the question: Do I have a soul that is separate from what religions think of as soul? If your answer is yes, then I invite you to define how you see your "soul" in such a way as you might recognize how it may serve you in your daily life.

Finally, I challenge readers to come to terms with questions they may have about their own immortality. Do you truly believe in an afterlife? Are you glad about the possibility of living millions years into infinity somewhere in a place in the sky called heaven? Can you accept that you may have only one life, the one you are having right here, and right now on this Earth?

These questions are examined in greater detail in the chapters ahead. Be open to your natural spiritual life that is within, even though these experiences are likely to be quite different from the traditions of your religion. One thing we might all agree upon is that it is worthwhile to work together in building Heaven on Earth. Such cooperative efforts arise from our sacred human spirit, and are the driving force serving humanity.

CHAPTER ONE

Making The Supernatural Natural

Imagine there's no heaven, it's easy if you try
No hell below us, above us only sky
Imagine all the people, living for today . . .
—John Lennon

I imagine that John Lennon is right—no hell below us, above us only sky! But according to Christians, this is not the way it is! They insist that heaven is in the skies and that we will meet God there and see Jesus, and so on. But here on Earth, we can see and hear and feel and touch heaven, as we engage in the process of building better lives for all of earth's creatures. In the human realm, most of us know that we want more democracy, less crime, more justice, and fewer wars. We know that we must reverse the massive starvation and malnutrition that affect millions, and that means figuring out how to distribute Earth's abundant resources in an equitable manner. It also means summoning the will to do it. This is a spiritual matter.

Letting Go

Over the last two millennia, millions if not billions of Christians bought into and held onto the idea of a supernatural *God as a human figure wearing a robe, and living in the skies above.* Today's Christians continue these beliefs, having faith that after they die on earth, they will meet God in Heaven in an afterlife. All that is required is that they believe in Jesus and repent their sins. Christians, who continue to have faith in their stories, will feel threatened by the idea of letting go of these and other supernatural beliefs. But being good Christians, they also know that humans can't let greed or anything else stand as a viable reason for neglecting to help those who are less fortunate. As *'good Samaritans'*, they too will contribute in helping to build heaven on earth, because it is the right thing to do. But for many of these who are devoutly religious, it will not be easy to let *go of their beliefs in supernatural ideas.* They may consider that their work for the common good has nothing to do with heaven, except that it might help when their credentials are reviewed for entrance to Heaven.

Letting go of supernatural ideation does not mean that anyone has to give up believing in God as a higher power. It just means accepting the truth that any explanation of any God is a mystery. Believing in a natural God does not explain the why what and how of it all, just as nothing is truly explained by any of religions mythological stories in that regard.

The difficult thing for those who believe in an afterlife is being able to accept the idea that when all the cellular tissues of our physical bodies have perished and gone to gravesites or crematoriums, we are gone, and life is over. Most people just do not want their lives to be over, and some religions have created supernatural stories that give them comfort that all is not gone. Whether one believes in a Natural God or the God of any religion, the common ground is that God is still seen as the abiding *Force* in the Universe and of life on Earth. The big difference is that a Natural God is seen as within as well as without, and needs no supernatural stories to explain the mystery. Believing in a Natural God means that we accept that the mystery is beyond anything that we can fathom, never mind making up stories to explain it. The interesting paradox of this mystery is that we are a part of it all. The mystery is within us at all times, as well as all around us. It is the spark, the breath and the force within all life.

While it will not be easy to shift ones belief in a supernatural God to believe in a Natural God, it may help one in considering such a shift, to be reminded that everything we need to build heaven on earth can be found in the abundance, beauty, and love that are plentiful in our natural world.

A Natural Force of Creation

If God is a natural Force, and the source for creation of all that we can perceive on earth, we have to conclude that *whatever this creative force is, we are part and parcel of it all.* This force is not contained in some outside supernatural *being* in a remote and vague place called heaven. Being one with nature is a much more direct connection to the total texture, movement, and interrelatedness of all life on Earth. To imagine a supernatural God in human form as a biological being, male, or female figure ruling over everything, does not make sense to me, especially one who is being called upon everyday to answer millions of individual prayers.

No religion has the final word on God or everlasting life, and it is arrogant to claim to understand such a mystery by offering supernatural stories. Religions get around and sidetrack this deficiency by simply saying that *'God works in mysterious ways.'* That explanation usually lets them off the hook, even though it tells us nothing. These folks continue to imply that other than the way *he* works, they understand everything about their supernatural God. This strikes me as dishonest.

Religions Rules

Most religions instruct followers to have *faith* in their claim that God is a supernatural being residing in heaven, even though there is no evidence supporting that idea, they tell all who will listen. They also tell us that during our lifetime we may connect with our 'Heavenly Father' only through prayer, and we all find out soon enough that these prayers may not be answered. *He* may get back to us, and *he* may not. I believe that if something good happens *and* we have been praying, it is because we made it happen by listening to our soul self of God within.

My challenges to religions do not stem from an atheistic point of view. It's not that I don't believe in a Higher Power; it is that I don't believe in religions that portray God as a human figure with supernatural backdrops of angels flying in the sky with their own wings, and with Saint Peter waiting at the heavenly gates to check the credentials of those seeking entrance. Why would there be a God who is so exclusive and judgmental?

Could this be religion's way of scaring us into behaving properly? Likewise, I fail to see value in other worn-out irrelevancies in religious stories and admonitions. Some of the Christian stories, such as the virgin birth, Jesus walking on water, or Jesus raising the dead, are examples of what were probably intended to be metaphors, but are presented and believed by the faithful to be reality. This is a huge distortion, and we know it can't be true. These metaphorical and mythological distractions do not help us find the truth.

Because most religions assert that their God is the only true God, they separate themselves from any and all who are of a different persuasion. In their separateness, religions condemn us and threaten us with damnation if in their judgment we have sinned. None of these judgments or threats will ever be considered if one believes in a Natural God. The mysteries of the universe and the inexplicable diversity of life on Earth are too extraordinary to be judged, defined, or contained within the walls of any religion that is built on supernatural myths.

While we all struggle to understand the *why* of these mysteries, it is reasonable to assume that the diversity of life on Earth is an outcome of a Natural Force that we might call Creator, God, or a Higher Power. Accepting the mystery and the wonder at the vastness of our Universe, and the natural beauty and abundance of life on Earth, we might conclude that *the ground upon which we stand is sacred.* We will see that our spiritual experiences are not just found in the rituals, artifacts, and traditions of our churches, temples, or mosques, nor are they only found in the isolated events that are reserved for special days of religious service. Instead, our experiences of the sacred are found within the textures of our daily relationships with our families and friends. These are the connections that enrich our lives in the here and now. There is no evidence that this vitality within our spiritual life will be found in some paradise in the sky reserved for life after death for those that are allowed in.

Living Without Fixed Answers

Religions like fixed answers. Without fixed answers, we are left to wonder. We wonder about God, about the meaning of our life, and about the mystery of our universe. Religions have not encouraged us to wonder.

They have provided fixed answers to discourage the uncertainty of the wondering path. But it is in our wondering that we discover that there is no exactitude in defining the parameters of the Force of God. This mystery will remain. It is in this wondering that we discover comfort in accepting and living with the mystery. And in our wondering, we open doors to understanding the meaning of our lives.

These are serious questions about our existence. Wondering awakens our consciousness, and we begin to realize that we can at least make some reasonable assumptions about what we are doing here, and how it came to be. For example, we easily realize that each of us comes from a long genealogical family tree, and we are connected to that heritage. We also come to see that although we belong to a community of friends with a culture and history, our own fate rests with our self-understanding as we consider our best options and make the decisions that will shape our lives. Fixed answers will not help us on this path.

Our Evolving Consciousness

As our consciousness rises, we begin to understand the nature of our soul. Claiming our *soul* means discovering our interface with the Natural Force of God within. It is our soul that is the seat of our spirit, our vitality, and our consciousness. Our soul consciousness integrates our perception, analysis, and reasoning from which we take meaning as we meet life's challenges. This integration forms the wisdom of our intuition, our greatest resource as we choose our way on life's journey.

A down to earth example of this idea may be seen in the following metaphorical piece about the uncertain consequences of decision-making. The following lines were written by Robert Frost, one of America's greatest poets, and are taken from his well-known poem, "The Road Not Taken."

I shall be telling this with a sigh
Somewhere ages and ages hence:
Two roads diverged in a wood, and I—

I took the one less traveled by,
And that has made all the difference.

One might say that his intuition, or the inner wisdom of his soul, told him to take that particular road because of a sense that his outcomes might just be a bit better (more interesting, more opportunities, safer, whatever). He trusted his sensing of it, his choice, and seems to be telling us that he is pleased by the enormity of the differences that ensued.

New Frontiers

In the last couple of centuries, there have been a few priests, ministers, rabbis, and mullahs that have challenged the rigidity of their own religion's particular storyline and protocol. John O'Donahue, the late Irish priest and author of several books of philosophical poetic musings on Celtic spirituality, provides a good example of this when he wrote the following in his book *Anam Cara* (translated "Soul Friend"): "For too long, we have believed that the divine is outside us."[1]

This twelve-word message is what this book is all about. It's about believing the divinity of our inner world, and the freedom we gain when we leave the traditional focus of a divinity outside ourselves that holds us back. It is not really probable for most established major religions to encourage us to look within to the force of a Natural God. Instead, they rein us in tightly to their point of view, suggesting that our earthly life is only a preview, and insisting that if we repent, everlasting life will be ours after we die. It is this centuries old devotion to supernatural stories perpetrated by major religions that continues to be a barrier to the understanding of our individual spirituality.

---

[1] John O'Donahue, *Anam Cara: Spiritual Wisdom from the Celtic World* (Uxbridge: Bantam Press, 1997), p. 84.

Freedom to Choose

Those of us not affiliated with religion will be judged, but we need not be diminished by this judgment, nor should we feel shy about claiming our freedom to choose what we believe. We need not be concerned with labels such as heretic, atheist, and pagan, which are often thrown at us by the most judgmental (holier than thou) and dogmatic folks of our religious cultures. It is their attempt to shame us into conforming. Our personal beliefs about God are too important to be invalidated by any outside judgment. We should not allow it. We are all spiritual beings by nature, and being spiritual does not require membership in any religion. *God simply does not belong to any religion!*

Accepting the Mystery

There will always be mystery in the millions of things we cannot understand. Certainly the mystery of the universe is at the very core of being awe struck with wonder. But even with all the mystery, there are hundreds of thousands of things that we can observe and do, that bring us delight in our wondering. These are the things that help us find meaning in our own lives. We will never fully grasp the immensity of our cosmos, but we can experience our awareness of self, as we embrace our bountiful Earth with reverence. Every day should be one in which we stand in awe at the infinite variety, abundance, and beauty of life as the gifts that they are. For me it makes sense simply to accept this inexplicable mystery and the wonder of it all. I am filled with gratitude and reverence for every breath I take and every step I make. There are so many possibilities.

Ask yourself if you can accept the idea that the Force of a Higher Power is the source of the creation of all living things. Can you accept that this life-giving Force is in our DNA, the blueprint of our cellular structure? Might we dare to think that God is the Force within us that directs our adaptability? Can we deny that our consciousness, cognition, and temperament—all the subtle yet profound nuances of our behavior—are the result of this adaptive force of natural selection within us? Could any person say that our creation is not sacred?

It is truly humbling to consider the astonishing Force in the universe that has created our rich, diverse, and abundant life, with an exquisitely ordered moon and sun supporting this beautiful planet we call home. Mary Oliver captures the spirit and essence of this in her following poem.[2]

The Summer Day

Who made the world?
Who made the swan and the black bear?
Who made the grasshopper?
This grasshopper, I mean-
The one who has flung herself out of the grass
The one who is eating sugar out of my hand,
Who is moving her jaws back and forth instead of up and down—
Who is gazing around with her enormous and complicated eyes.
Now she lifts her pale forearms and thoroughly washes her face.
Now she snaps her wings open, and floats away.
I don't know exactly what a prayer is.
I do know how to pay attention, how to fall down into the grass, how to kneel down in the grass, how to be idle and blessed, how to stroll through the fields, which is what I have been doing all day.
Tell me, what else should I have done?
Doesn't everything die at last, and too soon?
Tell me what you plan to do with your one wild and precious life.

---

[2]   Mary Oliver, *New and Selected Poems* (Cambridge: Beacon Press, 1992).

CHAPTER TWO

Life On Earth Is All We Know

Earth's the right place for love:
I don't know where it is likely to go better.
—Robert Frost, "Birches"

Here and Now

One can sense the reverence that Robert Frost had for life on Earth and for the interconnectedness of love between humans. We have made a start on building heaven on Earth, but we are a long way from being finished. We know very well that life on Earth can be a living hell for far too many people, and that there is much to do to create well being and opportunities for all to thrive.

John F. Kennedy said in his inaugural address, "For here on Earth, God's work must truly be our own." This particular statement has resonated with me as a deep truth for more than fifty years. This straightforward and powerful phrase helps me to see that the Force of a Natural God is in our own hands.

We have been conditioned by our religions to see God's work as that which is done by a distant and all powerful deity in the sky. In doing this we have taken ourselves out of the equation, and fail to claim the force of a natural God within that will guide us to take responsibility for building heaven on earth.

The Abundance of Earth

Science tells us that our sun is one of three hundred billion suns in our galaxy, and that our galaxy is one of one hundred billion galaxies! It is an unfathomably vast universe. And here we are awestruck on this beautiful blue planet we call home and a bit dumbfounded by the mystery of it all. We take solace as we ground ourselves to find our way with balance and perspective here on Earth. We take comfort and reassurance in knowing that the sun will rise every morning and that the seasons will roll around with orderly and predictable precision. Earth is well endowed with all the resources for sustaining life. Everything we need on Earth is right here, and right now. Even as we attend to the suffering of those less fortunate, we need to be grateful for the progress made on many fronts and for the generosity and the love we receive from others.

Omar Khayyam, the Persian poet-philosopher, who wrote so eloquently of the truth of our many blessings, telling us more than eight centuries ago that paradise is here and now. In his book . . . *The Rubaiyat*, he speaks of our abundance in paradise in his most well known piece below.

Here with a Loaf of Bread beneath the Bough
A Flask of Wine, a Book of Verse—and Thou
Beside me singing in the Wilderness
And Wilderness is Paradise now[3]

The Gift of Quiet Moments

One can feel the sensuous and joyous celebration of life on Earth in those four lines. We all need to give ourselves the gift of quiet moments in nature, in the mountains, at the desert, on a lake, or at the seashore, taking time to reflect, and to . . .

---

[3]   This is probably the most well known poem from *The Rubaiyat of Omar Khayyam* (New York: Three Sirens Press, 1933). He wrote this book at the turning of the 11th and 12th century in his native Persia.

- Listen to birds and other creatures express their songs
- Watch the sun and moon rise and set
- Experience the roar of thunder, the amazing force of lightning, and the revolving cleansing and nourishing of the Earth in never-ending cycles of rain and snow.
- Sit by a campfire as all of our ancestors have done
- Watch your children play, then fall asleep in your arms
. . . It would be a shame to miss any of it!

We all can experience the above in our earthly existence if we are open to seeing the natural gifts that are truly sacred in our daily lives. What need have we to consider angels with wings when there are so many wingless human angels here in front of us who are willing to help?

Lies about the Afterlife

We have been told by the Christian and Islamic faiths, to believe that there must be something more of life after we die. Christians believe that heaven is the place where all of our loved ones that have died have gone. Many believe they might even catch a glimpse of JFK or Abraham Lincoln, or better yet, Jesus, in that place in the sky called heaven.

Steve Jobs, one of the great creative technology minds of our time, reminded us in his address to Stanford University's Graduation address in 2005, "Even people who believe in an afterlife don't want to die." Of course that makes good sense, but why is it that people who want to live forever don't seem to be comfortable with just having one life to live? Is it because they have unfinished business? Do they want a second chance at life to clear up all the mistakes they may have made or another opportunity to experience all the omissions they chose to miss here on Earth?

Have they thought about living a million or ten million years? Have they considered that it might be boring, and that there doesn't seem much likelihood of making love, playing golf, dancing, singing, sailing, etc. Do they stop to think about wearing clothes? Driving cars or boats? Where would they get these? Would they have a body that is ageless? Would they grow older? Is there a Wal-Mart in heaven? Would they get sick or hurt or ever get a toothache? Would they eat food and have to eliminate? Would they get angry if someone they thought was a friend walked away to go greet a more famous person on the streets of heaven? Of course, these things are all too silly to consider since their physical bodies have turned to dust or ash. Why would people want to live such an unexamined life?

Again, the wisdom of Omar Khayyam reminds us of the importance of now and the folly of putting-off living life on Earth to the fullest:

Make the most of what we yet may spend
Before we to unto Dust Descend
For Dust unto Dust, and under Dust to lie,
Sans Wine, sans Song, sans Singer and sans end!

Contrast this bit of wisdom with a piece written more than a thousand years earlier in John 3:16 of the New Testament, where Christians are told the following about life.

For God so loved the world that he gave his only begotten son that whosoever believeth in him shall not perish but have everlasting life.

How is it that religions claim such an inordinate amount of power and inside information about God and eternity? My concern is that many people who belong to a religion have just gone along with this idea of an afterlife and never really questioned religion's authority to claim it as so. Nor have Christians questioned why their God would sacrifice his only begotten son. What kind of a God is this? We are all sons and daughters begotten by the mystery of the Force of God. Why is just one man by the name of Jesus singled out by God as the perfect being, and then allowed to be murdered, and martyred, by having him hang on a cross next to two thieves? This idea is too bizarre, but we are told that it is God's master plan.

Humans should not depend on outrageous claims such as reincarnation and other ethereal superstitions, where prophecies are channeled through cards, crystal balls, or tea leaves. Everything we know in life rails against such ideas. Just because religion tells us that our "soul" will survive after our biological body has died, does not mean that it is true? How is it that one's "soul" can have a life without any biological functions and sensory perception? No eyes, no ears, no bones, flesh, heart, brain, larynx, or lungs to draw a breath. Living demands that we have a complete and integrated biological system, so forget such nonsense as an afterlife without a biological body! Religions need to get real if they are going to survive in any relevant way into the twenty-first century. A huge part of that realness is to bring the utopian metaphor of heaven out of the skies and down to our tangible Earth, where it belongs.

Our Spirit Lives On in the Lives of Others

The only afterlife that makes any sense is that our spirit will live on in the lives of those we have touched in significant ways. A good example of this in my own life is my brother Loren, who died three years ago of complications from leukemia. I am reminded of him almost every day. His spirit is with me when I find myself laughing, gesturing, or otherwise using little expressions that I assimilated. In my early teenage years, I enjoyed just being around him and admired the way he coped with life.

I had a dream about him just the other night. He was sprinting the one-hundred-yard dash at full speed. In my dream he had thick black hair and the body of a twenty-year-old athlete. What a great dream, and it was so real! Still in my life, the legacy of his spirit lives on now in many of the ways I cope with life, as well as in my dreams. He was my real-life hero—an honor student and a great athlete. I remember one high school football game where he scored four touchdowns. I was the water boy for the team and was bursting with pride for my big brother. At the end of that season he went on to be selected to the All-Conference Team. In the early 1950s, He was among the first group of Navy pilots to take off, fly, and land jet fighter planes on aircraft carriers.

Loren earned his PhD and became a well-respected professor by his colleagues, as well as the many hundreds of students whom he taught at Western Washington State University for more than thirty-five years. Twice he was selected as the Outstanding Professor at the University. He was well loved by family and friends alike because his spirit touched all whom he met. I was very fortunate to be his kid brother. To say that he made a significant difference in shaping my life would be an understatement.

When his medical doctor diagnosed him, Loren was told that he had just a few months to live. He continued to set a high standard for courage and grace as he faced death with serenity, telling me, "Dwight, it's not so bad knowing that I'm going to die soon. It gives me time to say good-bye to my family and friends and to put my papers and such in some kind of order." When I asked him about his bucket list, he told me that he had already done everything he wished for, and then some. He said, "I'm ready to go. I'm grateful that I've had such a glorious and wonderful life!" Four months later, and just a month into his seventy-ninth year, he passed away with graceful acceptance. His last days were peaceful and his spirit grateful, with the same positive attitude he held throughout his life. This kind of immortality is built on the love we share with others as we pass through.

In that same vein, I received a great message on my Father's Day card this year from my son John. It touched my soul when he added a note that said, "By choosing to be an integral part of my life, by imparting your wisdom and knowledge, I believe you had the belief that the hugest of hugs, and praises of pride would carry on to the next generation. I am pleased to report they have, and they will."

Of course I will die, just as everyone else who lives will die, but for now I am focused on celebrating living. I am confident that my life continues to be well spent with the love of my family, my friends, my students, and those unmet souls who have written to tell me that they have appreciated reading something that I wrote. I am very grateful for so many who have loved me and shared their lives with me. Our spirits have connected, and many of those who have touched my soul remain a part of my life, showing up in a dream, or some flash of memory image that can still put a smile on my face, even though we are miles and sometimes years apart.

And so it is, I go on with life and love, nourished by the abundance of my blessings and the rich memories of sharing laughter and song, as well as sharing the hard times and tears with so many others along the way.

Grounding Utopian Dreams

Heaven has been created by religions as a way to assuage our fear of death. It represents our hopes for a better world and is a metaphor for a utopian dream. But heaven is not some station in the sky or a paradise in la-la land. It is being created here on Earth right now, one step at a time. Imagine heaven as a place where we live out our daily lives. It will evolve with our enlightenment guiding our experiences of compassion, kindness, respect, and forgiveness. These are some of the key spiritual ways of being that support our goal of living what it means to be fully human. Bringing these qualities into our lives are the conscious choices we make as we live our lives with more meaning than just taking care of business. The heart of our existence is in honoring the truth that we are here to serve our families and communities with our most sacred acts of love.

CHAPTER THREE

The Emperor Is Naked

We make our world significant
By the courage of our questions
And by the depth of our answers
—Carl Sagan[4]

Not questioning religion is a little bit like not questioning the Emperor's new clothes. As I remember that story . . .

> *The Emperor was riding through the village on his horse and was quite naked in the saddle. Because it had been announced in advance that he would be wearing his new suit of clothes, the adults pretended his nakedness could not be true and they all whispered lies amongst themselves. They commented, "Doesn't the Emperor have on a fine suit of clothes?" All the adults agreed that the Emperor looked wonderful in his new suit. It took the innocence of a child to loudly observe and announce the truth. "But the Emperor does not have any clothes on at all. He is naked!" said the lad.*

Religions have likewise paraded their myths and messages as truths as their leaders ride upon their high horses through the many villages and countries on the planet. Their nakedness is in their pretense that they have the final answers. Like the adults in the story of the naked Emperor, faithful followers have not questioned the myths and stories of established

---

[4]   Carl Sagan, *The Varieties of Scientific Experience* (New York: Penguin Press, 2006), 248.

religions. They realize that it is safer, and much more comfortable, to remain silent than it is to call out the truth and risk negative judgment and ostracism from family and friends. It is not just the faithful followers who play it safe; we are all aware of the importance of getting along within our community. As a result of our silence, religions have ridden their high horses for centuries, safe in the knowledge that they can count on the traps of conformity to appease those who might question the falseness of any part of their doctrines, scriptures, or traditions. When we choose to remain in the presence of irrelevancies, we reveal our fear and our failure to stand up for the truth.

One person who did stand up for the truth early in my career was Alan Watts, a popular philosopher of the 1960's and 1970's generation. He was a presenter at Esalen East, a three-day program in New York City, and his talk was brilliant. He introduced his presentation by telling the audience that he would play the part of a paranoid schizophrenic patient in a hospital, and we would all be medical staff members there. He explained, "Your job will be to convince me that I am not God, and I dare say that you will not be able to do that." He told us that we could ask him anything. I was the first to raise my hand and asked him, "Am I God also?"

He answered, "Of course."

I said, "No more questions," understanding his implication that we all carry the force of God within.

After his presentation I asked him why he did not go public with his belief that God was within us all. He replied, "Because I don't want to be crucified." Although I could imagine the real dangers of rejection and ostracism that he must have considered when deciding whether to go public, I was disappointed with his reply. I clearly wanted him to blaze the trail for me, because I did not feel ready for it. Now, at this stage of my life, forty years later, the danger of silence far outweighs my fear of rebuke. In fact, I feel compelled to challenge those statements made by religions that I believe can't be true.

Taking the Easy Way Out

Throughout history, religions have presented a supernatural God to their followers, and established norms with powerful influence on their respective cultures. We do not question these mythological stories and traditions, because to criticize one's religion is not acceptable. There are ready-made clichés in our culture that tell us, "Don't make waves," "Some things are best left alone," and "Let sleeping dogs lie." In conforming to such injunctions as these, the status quo remains undisturbed, and *we fail to muster the courage to speak our mind, settling instead for what we know can't be true.* It is when we walk the safe path that that we stifle our personal awareness by remaining silent. In so doing, we compromise the wisdom of our soul, and this is a very high price to pay. But considering the consequences of judgment and rejection that result from challenging the cultural norms and traditions, most of us are willing to pay that price. We relinquish our souls to our religions for safekeeping, because it is less threatening. I, like so many others, have *quietly* held-in my disbeliefs over the years, sailing along in the normative mainstream as a passive skeptic. I have been fearful of putting my thoughts on these matters into the public record, thinking that those faithful to their religions would judge me harshly. The irony of such judgment is enough to shake one's faith for sure.

Raised as a Christian in the protestant traditions, by the time I was a teenager, I concluded that the rules for believing and having faith were too confining, too confusing, and too exclusive and judgmental for me. The idea of a vengeful God, one who will not allow me into heaven if I am not a member of this or that particular religion, or if I have sinned and not repented, is an idea that never made sense to me. Fear of judgment, with an emphasis on sin and guilt, are dark clouds that I choose not to have hanging over my head. Religions, by their nature, promote intolerance and exclusion of those of a different persuasion. They tell us that their way is the right way, and they don't stop there—they tell us it is the *only* way. Such arrogant judgment only serves to further separate us from each other. I am certain that I am not alone in my distress with these failings of religions. These negative aspects of religions have turned me toward believing in the force of a Natural God, and I am certain that I am not alone in this. A recent poll reported that while 97 percent of Americans believed in God, only 67 percent claimed to be religious. This information gave me confidence on where I stand on these issues when I consider that every third person on the planet might believe in a Natural God, as I do, rather than the supernatural gods offered by most religions.

God Does Not Belong to Religion

Where is it written that in order to believe in God, we must belong to a religion that claims that God is the founder and author of that religion? How can any religion make such claims? I choose not to follow any religion, but this does not mean that I don't have a belief about a God as a Higher Power, a Creator, or some other magnificent and inexplicable natural force by any name. Our lives are too amazing simply to dismiss the idea of a natural God with jaded atheism. Part of our evolution as humans is our rising consciousness. We have become able to see ourselves as spiritual beings as we consider our relationship to the Universe, and to all of life, with a sense of wondering: "How did all this come to be"?

As passengers on planet Earth, we are passing through space toward an unknown destination, and for unknown reasons. In spite of these and other mysteries, our spirituality alerts our curiosity, imagination, inventiveness, wonder, passion, and gratitude among thousands of other avenues through which we express the vitality of our life. I am totally comfortable in accepting the mystery of what life is all about, and am humbled by the magnificence of the natural world that supports all of life. To be grateful for being alive is to recognize a force for good that is manifesting throughout this inexplicable journey.

While evil remains among our human experiences, the greater human force on this planet is for the common good. It is our spiritual energy that reveals the spark of life that is within us as we experience compassion and caring in our mutual nurturing with kindred spirits. There is laughter to balance the tears, and there is hope and joy to overcome the cynicism of selfish greed and corruption.

Major religions do not emphasize that God is within, and they do not encourage followers to pursue this path. Instead, they tell us that God is in heaven and that it is our task is to get to heaven to be with Him and to have eternal life. They have taught us to pray to an omnipotent God-Being and ask Him for forgiveness for our sins and for guidance in His path of righteousness. This is an external God-figure who religions tell us will give special personal consideration and favors to individuals who follow His ways and pray faithfully to Him. Religions have led us down this path, claiming to be the sole custodians of our spiritual lives. They continuously remind us that they will take care of matters of our soul and spirit, and we learn from conventional wisdom that clearly says, "Hands off! Don't even think about talking about spirituality outside the context of religions! To do so would be a sacrilege!" They have led us down the wrong path.

The fact is, *we are spiritual beings whether or not we belong to any religion.* It is our inherent spiritual essence that has formed religions, and not the other way around. Religions have simply taken the reins and harnessed our natural spiritual inclinations to the wagons of their domain. Religions have claimed that what is sacred in life is that which occurs in the ceremonies of churches, temples, and mosques that celebrate and honor the history and traditions of our culture. These messages are delivered with their prayers, doctrines, rituals, hymns, and scriptures, when their services are held on special days that are set aside for worship.

We have yielded to religions definition of what is spiritual and become so conditioned to this way of being that when most people think of spirituality, they automatically couple it with religion. Religions like this pairing, because it adds fuel to their tank. In plain and simple truth, spirituality and religion are not synonymous. And true allegiance of our spirit to any institution can only be invited, never required. Spirituality, by its very nature, does not owe allegiance to any institution, for it is a personal and individual matter. In contrast, religions are a group experience and have survived because people are inclined to gather and join in groups. There is strength in numbers, and there is an innate longing to belong to a community of like-minded individuals.

For more than a few thousand years, religions have held a tight grip on our spiritual lives in the diverse religious cultures on our planet. Most people have gone along with this tradition, and allowing their spirituality to be defined by their religions. Today, we are entering a time when we see that there is room for personal choices. This growing awareness of our individual freedom opens the door for us to ask ourselves to define our own inherent spirituality.

People are *finding it easier to leave their religious institutions* as they discover that many of the ways of ancient religions are irrelevant and some even evil. This includes the self-serving greed and ostentatious displays of wealth in houses of worship, as well as the criminal behavior of Catholic priests, who have preyed upon children for generations. In addition, as the Information Age unfolds, we have come to see that most major religions have given both overt and covert political support for wars, genocide, and killing. This is a very big part of religion's nakedness, and it is currently being exposed as we challenge the denial and under-the-rug sweeping of such activities.

It has become clear that many of the ancient scriptures are in opposition to the values of our times. Many such scriptures are contradictory to the idea that all life is sacred. If religions are going to survive in some reasonable way, they will need to examine their relevancy and their values in today's world, and they must determine if there are in fact some doctrines and traditions that could be respectfully laid to rest in the archives of museums to serve as examples from our earlier history.

The Soul Connection

I encourage you to look within yourselves and become acquainted with your own soul, for it is your soul connection that will help you to tap into the force and wisdom of your inner spirit. Your soul is your inner guide and your most important voice in making choices that are in your best interest and for creating outcomes in your lives that will move you toward fulfilling your potential. Going within to check with your innermost soul-self, is a process that will require you to take full responsibility for how you choose to be.

Apple founder Steve Jobs said in his address to the graduates of Stanford University's class of 2005: "Your time is limited, so don't waste it living someone else's life. Don't be trapped by dogma—which is living with the results of other peoples thinking. Don't let the noise of other's opinions drown out your own inner music. And most importantly, have the courage to follow your heart and intuition. They somehow already know what you truly want to become. Everything else is secondary."

Dwight Webb, PhD

A Natural God Is a Bridge to Science

Both science and religion present themselves as polar opposites. But why must there be this polarity? By positing that God is a Natural Force, I am challenging this traditional and rigid viewpoint. A Natural God is the bridge that aligns spirituality with science. I suggest that what we may call God, or a Higher Power, is the source of creation and is also the force that is embedded in our DNA. *This is the driving force of evolution, the most continuing creative act on Earth.* It is the source of all of biology, all the pulsating life springing forth from the beginnings of life that emerged from primordial ooze.

The eminent biologist and proclaimed atheist, Richard Dawkins tells us "the genetic code is in fact literally identical in all animals, plants and bacteria that have ever been looked at. All earthly things are certainly descended from a single ancestor."[5]

But this is not merely a God gene about which I am writing; it is the creative force that permeates the totality of the genetic makeup of all life. If we can accept that this might be the case, it follows that the creative force of God does not just exist in one's mind or one's heart but rather in every cell in every living organism, and is the foundation of life itself.

Human consciousness plays an important role in this evolution by allowing us to make a connection with *wonder* as we consider the mystery of the universe. Consciousness leads us to become more aware of our spiritual essence, and we begin to question the need for interventions by religions and their intermediaries that serve to connect humans with God. Most of these intermediaries are men, and many are so caught up in their own "holiness" and sense of entitlement that their mission is severely impaired. How is it that so many priests who are blatant criminals in their sexual predation are allowed to continue to serve, representing themselves as intermediaries to help others with spiritual concerns? Their pious self-righteousness and self-proclaimed authority is a lie! What about a God without criminal messengers, without myths, uniforms, and dogma? What about a God as a force within each life? Is this not in the realm

---

5   Biologist Richard Dawkins makes these assertions in many of his books. These particular quotes are from *The River of Eden: A Darwinian View of Life* (New York, Perseus Books, 1995), 12.

of possibility? We should not throw a Natural God out with the dirty bathwaters of religion.

Our consciousness also allows us to see that *religions are but one avenue to express our spirituality.* There are many other avenues, such as meditation, yoga, communing with nature, music, art, astrology, and other mystical, esoteric, and unique traditions, as well as individual or non-traditional beliefs, such as belief in a Natural God. While we may conclude that God does not belong to religions or cults, we see in every culture that religions have been the primary choice for people to file their spirituality. And therein lies the problem: *their spirituality is filed.*

If we are to claim our spirituality, we need to take it out of our files, and personally get to work in discovering ways to come to terms with how our spirit may be expressed in our individual daily lives on Earth. When we do this, we will redefine God in the context and meaning of our own lives.

Here is a brief summary example of important differences between spirituality and religion.

Differences between Spirituality and Religion

Religion	Spirituality
Organized in groups	Individual experience
Absolute authority	Open beginners mind
Myths and rituals	Grounded in everyday life
Reward is everlasting life	Reward is here and now
God is a separate being	God is within all life
God is vengeful	God is love
Scripture is word of God	Viewpoints are authored by humans
Unquestioning devotion	Thoughtful inner searching

Religions represent a point of view about God as the *Father*. They deal with answers of how the world began and how we should act and be in it so that we can please God. Within their bureaucratic institutions, they tell us that heaven is in the skies and that we should behave ourselves. They instruct us that we should be true believers if we are to get ourselves ready for eternity. These points of view have changed very little over hundreds of generations.

In spite of these claims by religion it is imperative to understand and acknowledge that we are all spiritual beings, even though we may or may not believe in or choose to belong to any religion. Separating ourselves from religion does not mean separating ourselves from our spiritual essence, nor does it mean that we are separating ourselves from our belief in God.

Groupthink and the Dangers of Membership

The danger of belonging to any religion as an avenue to spirituality is that it will involve membership in a group that could have very rigid beliefs. The rules are set, the answers are fixed, and members tend to back away from taking further responsibility for exploring their spiritual lives. They will instead rely on fixed formats, programs, and procedures. Rigid bureaucracies invite closing doors, not opening doors. If we abandon our spirit (the most sacred essence of our lives), we derail our personal quest for meaning. Loyal followers have yielded to the institution for taking care of their spiritual matters.

We humans have been surprisingly passive in yielding the care of our soul to others, and this passivity squelches our natural urge for growth. Our job is to actively search. Here are some of the searching matters of our human spirit that I weave into the fabric of this book.

- Knowing that our best self is found within our own life force that seeks health and balance.
- Discovering that our meaning and purpose will make our world a better place for all.

- Finding that inner peace and the ability to express love are essential if we are to actualize our potential, and gain a sense of reverence and gratitude toward all of life.

As we consider how we might be stuck in the rigid traditions and ceremonies of religion, we will begin to take responsibility for defining and clarifying our own beliefs about what our spiritual life is and can be. In so doing, we will cease to give power to institutions to define and/or judge us as we claim, perhaps for the first time, the truth that spirituality is the essence of our humanity.

CHAPTER FOUR

Down The Wrong Path

This is my simple religion. There is no need for temples; no need for
complicated philosophy.
Our own brain, our own heart is our temple; philosophy is kindness.
—Dali Lama

Religions have meant well, but their ancient iterations have led us away from the development of our inner spirit. Christianity, for example, has told us that we are part of God's special flock, and that we should behave ourselves or we will experience damnation and hellfire or some other suitable punishment for our sins. The faithful have taken in these stories and threats lock, stock, and barrel, as the word of God, and as such may not be questioned! No challenges allowed. We remain mired in the traditions of a belief system that dates back to the Old Testament and the preceding centuries it took to form that document.

Yet religions are so embedded within the social fabric of their respective cultures that the faithful go along with the traditions of their families and their communities out of loyalty. It would be considered a sacrilege to go against the edicts of our churches, temples, and mosques. Even though we know that much of the writing of these early scriptures is not relevant for our time, we have not dared to challenge religions authority because we fear the social consequences of such an act.

The three major religions tell us *that God is a male human figure,* and accept this at some level, even while knowing that *no biological being* of any gender could have created the universe of galaxies stretching over billions of light years, nor could such a *being* have the supernatural power to create the balance of our own exquisite Earth, Sun, and Moon, and all the elements that support life on our planet. When we are told one thing

26

and believe it and at the same time know it can't be true, we are stuck in an incongruity. The fact that we have ignored this misalignment speaks to the strength of religious sanctions that shape the beliefs of the majority of our culture. We go along quietly, rather like an ostrich hiding his head in the ground, we choose not to question it or even look at the absurdity of it. We override our common sense about what is reasonable, because it is easier, and a lot less threatening, to go along and remain silent.

But why not ask questions and examine our own lives? Science can't fully explain this magnificent, pervasive, and creative force that we see unfolding before us. In spite of the fact that the mystery of it all is unknowable, it is reasonable to assume that there is *some ubiquitous force* upon which we are all interdependent and inextricably linked. All life forms are an outcome of this force.

Religions, by focusing on a God that is a separate being outside ourselves, have gently led us away from looking within. But it is our inner spirituality that is sacred not religions supernatural formats.

Humans Create Religions

We have made up stories about God and the great mystery of life since the dawning of our consciousness. In our quest for meaning, we have invented God, and we know from our recorded history that these stories begin to cohere along consistent themes within particular cultures. Believing in the stories creates cohesion and a sense of belonging among the faithful, and this cohesion has been enormously important for religions in becoming the dominant force for shaping the social fabric within their various cultures. We see this dominance in the religious expressions of music, painting, sculpture, and literature, throughout history.

In the Jewish, Christian, and Islamic religions, Moses, Jesus, and Mohammed, continue to be revered as iconic prophets by their respective followers. These prophets have become central figures in the developing doctrines, dogmas, rituals, and traditions of each. Over time, bureaucratic hierarchies evolved, and priests, ministers, rabbis, and mullahs would be trained to serve as intermediaries, transmitting their story about their God, all offering their own pathway to salvation. Throughout history, followers have accepted these intermediaries as men who would illuminate the correct path to God. No questions asked! Thus we witness the accomplishing of one of the primary tasks of each culture—transmitting itself to the next generation.

Not surprisingly, over the centuries these religious institutions developed certain rigidities to safeguard and conserve their traditions. Consider, for example, the Catholic male leadership hierarchy. We see authority descending from the Pope to the cardinals, archbishops, bishops, priests, deacons, and on down to ordinary laypeople, all conveniently perpetuating the myth of male superiority with a God favoring men for these leadership positions. Each religion has its own traditions, hierarchies, and rigidities, with some striving to offer more gender balance than the Catholics. In spite of these egalitarian efforts, most important positions in the leadership and administrative hierarchies of temples, churches, and mosques, are filled with males. How is it that religions can endow these men to be intermediaries to God? How is it that we just accept that this is the way it is supposed to be?

In light of this reality, we have to ask, *Why would humans create any religion with a God that would ask them to abuse and kill other humans?* Could it be that each tribe or culture wants God to be on its side to provide safety from the threats of their warring enemies? It is a dangerous delusion and superstition to believe that God would play favorites among religions by sending humans into killing wars on the chessboard of national and cultural allegiance to sort out which religion will win. This is essentially a question of human territorial greed and pride, with religions carrying the banners. We must not fail to own the fact that we have created and allowed this actuality to happen and to continue throughout history.

The Need for Answers

Humans want to have answers to questions that don't have answers, and religions are glad to offer answers that by cultural edict can't be challenged. These fixed answers help build common ground among people who are looking for leadership. So much the better if it comes from the all-powerful source of God. These answers provide followers with some comfort, as well as a sense of belonging within a larger community of kin and like-minded folks. Most religions wisely include theater, pageantry, ceremony, and prayers as a way of projecting reverence and confidence in their knowledge of God and the origins of life on Earth. The ultimate reward that Christian and Islamic religions offer is that the faithful get to go to heaven and have everlasting life if they follow the rules. Heaven is a perfect metaphor and answer for the mystery of it all. It is out of sight, and seems to lie somewhere just beyond our imagination in the vastness of the unknowable universe from which everything has been born, and to which everything must return.

The burdens of mystery and uncertainty are lifted for those who believe in the absolute authority of God as the Father, allowing them to see themselves as the children of God—another metaphor that can be dangerously misguiding when taken literally. But religions doctrines are offered as the literal truth, and to question their authority is a rude behavior that might earn one the label of heretic and the status of an outcast within the community.

Rejection by our community, our family, and our friends is an extremely painful social consequence. Humans have a powerful need for belonging, whether it is to our families, our peer friendship group, a team, a gang, or some other group in our lives that gives us comfort, identity, and meaning. Of course there is also a huge economic advantage in belonging to the conventional social fabric, with all its commercial connections. Conformity pays off big time. To express our doubts publicly with regard to the veracity of religions doctrines is to undermine our success on every front. In order to be safe and to be embraced within the belonging of our family and community, we go along in passive compliance with what our group believes. The downside of this *groupthink* is that it opens us to accept myths, and the ensuing fears and superstitions enmeshed with the faith. Believing in a judgmental God who resides in heaven, sees everything, knows everything, and can strike us down without a moment's notice if we are not faithful is a dark cloud designed to keep us on track by reminding us that the good and moral life depends on our adherence to the doctrines of our religions.

While these injunctions have in some ways been helpful for building a civil society, as we enter the twenty-first century we need to ask ourselves, "Are we are ready to challenge the history of our passive yielding? Is it possible that we could build a civil society without belonging to a religion? Might such a society even be more civil?"

Challenging Worn-Out Myths

The evidence from artifacts discovered by researchers in the fields of paleontology, archeology, geology, and related sciences tells us that the earliest *Homo sapiens* lived more than 4.1 million years ago. The stark truth of this evidential knowing completely erodes and demolishes the believability of the book of Genesis. In this first book of the Old Testament we are told that God created the world some six thousand years ago, doing it in six days. Then, seeing that is was good, *He* rested on the seventh day.

We can forgive the writers of those ancient scriptures for their lack of knowledge when we consider that the discoveries that have informed us today were not available to them. In those early times it must have been important for them to have a story that explained at least some of the mystery. But in this day and age, it is beyond reason to believe in the Bible's version of our origins. Our origins are too important to base their understanding on a fairytale written by people several thousand years ago. These were uneducated people who *needed* a father figure to worship, especially if *He* could supply answers to the mystery of it all. These early storytellers and writers of the scriptures from the dawning of recorded history did the best they could with what they could surmise, *but they were then, as we are now, trapped in a time capsule of their own culture.*

In spite of the overwhelming scientific evidence supporting the efficacy of evolution, a recent survey in the United States revealed that 40 percent of Americans believe the Genesis story of creation, and 70 percent believe this creation story should be taught in schools along with evolution. Daniel Dennett reminds us in his brilliant book *Darwin's Dangerous Idea* what a terrible offense is to misinform children.[6] One would think that when a light goes on we would see things more clearly and say good-bye to the darkness. But religions have a very strong grip.

---

[6]   Daniel Dennett, *Darwin's Dangerous Idea: Evolution and the Meaning of Life* (New York: Simon and Shuster, 1995).

We Perpetuate a History of Nonsense

If we look closely at the scriptures (those purported holy words to which most of us pay lip service), we will find many proclamations that are not only inaccurate but also grossly inappropriate and undeserving to be considered as the word of God in a civilized world. In some cases, they urge followers to do evil acts. Sam Harris, the author of *Letter to a Christian Nation*, speaks to this point when he lists some common and redundant themes that show up in the books of Proverbs, Leviticus, Deuteronomy, and even Mark and Mathew:

> "We must stone people to death for heresy, adultery, homosexuality, working on the Sabbath, worshipping graven images, practicing sorcery and a wide variety of other imaginary crimes."[7]

While these very early writings of scriptures tell us about the culture and traditions of their times, they no longer make sense in the twenty-first century. To embrace them puts us all in danger. To punctuate this danger, Harris helps us see the absurdity of the message he quotes from, Deuteronomy 13:6:

> "If your brother, the son of your mother, or your son, or your daughter or the wife of your bosom, or your friend who is as your own soul, entices you secretly saying 'Let us go and serve other Gods, you shall not yield to him or listen to him, nor shall your eye pity him, nor shall you spare him, nor shall you conceal him: but **you shall kill him**; your hand shall be first against him to put him to death, and afterward the hand of all people."[8]

---

[7] Sam Harris, *Letter to a Christian Nation* (New York: Vintage, 2008). On page 8, he quotes from Proverbs 13:24, 20:30, and 23:13–14, Levitucus 20–9, Deuteronomy 21:18–21, Mark 7:9–13 and Mathew 15:4–7.

[8] Ibid, 8, 9.

In spite of these grotesque proclamations, we have naively and unquestioningly accepted these ancient scriptures. If we can be honest with ourselves, we would admit to being grossly repelled by the arrogance and stupidity of such scriptures in our world today. Paying homage to edicts that call for the killing of family members or dearest friends could not be more absurd, and yet this killing practice continues today in some religious cultures. The fact that we have not challenged these scriptures or these practices is a powerful example of how successful religions have been in keeping us passive and compliant.

In earlier cultures, the authors of scriptures took it as their duty to protect their tribe from potential enemies. Each tribe used God as their figurehead to instill fear, create violence, punishments, vengeance, and wars, to keep their people safe and ready to fight should an external threat arise. These ancient scriptures were written to accommodate the needs, traditions, and beliefs, of their people, and to maintain cohesion in the culture at large. While we can understand this in the historical context of that time, we are long overdue in taking responsibility for rebuking and casting out these anachronistic and dangerous messages. These scriptures belong in museums as artifacts of human history.

These murderous scriptures from Judaism, Christianity, and Islamic traditions have handed down a common history of nonsense, and we perpetuate this practice by putting up with it. If this is the word of God, it's a fair question to ask: "What kind of a God is this?" In our culture today, this kind of a God is a mockery. It is an embarrassment to hold words that encourage killing as sacred. We should see this feeble claim for what it is, a product from the imaginations of an unenlightened and fearful people. No longer should we revere these scriptures as the foundation of our religious beliefs, which purport to be the word of God. We truly know better! Loyal and unthinking followers need to own their part in perpetuating this nonsense. One might wonder if the writers of these scriptures could have predicted that we would be following their irrelevancies into the twenty-first century.

This unquestioning adherence to religious doctrines continues to blind those who will not accept the truth even though they can see the absurdity and threat to all. This stubborn blindness continues to create barriers that separate people, contributes to mutual mistrust, and leads us into wars against each other. The religious genocide in Rwanda and the many conflicts in the Middle East and Afghanistan today are clear examples of how the madness of religions can cross over the edge of sanity. Religions that endow themselves with self-righteousness continue to be a major reason for the wars of ethnic cleansing and genocide that we experience in our own time.

If we are to adapt and survive as a species, we must not perpetuate these reciprocating cycles of revenge. These cultural atrocities belong to history. Greed, murder, rape, and plunder must no longer be excused under the banner of any religion. Certainly we cannot wish to continue down this path. Not in the name of any God are these bizarre acts acceptable. Such unquestioning loyalty is a dangerous state of being. Richard Dawkins points clearly to this danger when he writes,

> "Christianity, just as much as Islam teaches children that unquestioned faith is a virtue. If you belong to a religion, you don't have to make a case for what you believe. If somebody announces that it is part of his faith, the rest of society, whether the same faith, or another, or of none, is obliged by ingrained custom, to 'respect' it without question. Respect it until the day it manifests itself in a horrible massacre like the destruction of the World Trade Center, or the London or Madrid bombings."

Claiming Our Personal Courage to Challenge

In our passive deference and compliance we have allowed the churches, temples, and mosques to assume the authority to define what is sacred and dictate the boundaries and norms of our spiritual life. We have forfeited our courage and our freedom to challenge the myths and fixed answers by not daring to claim our own spiritual beliefs. The great loss from this forfeiture is that we have been conditioned to be unquestioning, and in so doing have impaired the integrity of our own spiritual development. This quiet, subtle, but huge abdication of our personal spiritual life to the institutions of religion has had far-reaching implications, not the least of which is our loss of voice, our forceful and spirited autonomy.

Religions that demand loyalty from followers who share their history and traditions stir up considerable trouble when they express the following attitude: "Our religion and the people in our culture are better than yours." This is the attitude and belief that declares, "God is on our side." For all readers interested in the implications for warfare in this regard, I refer you to Christopher Hitchens and Sam Harris, who both provide a more comprehensive overview with specific examples of how religions are often the root cause of wars.[9]

Any challenges to the traditions of religion will no doubt be dismissed by loyal followers as heretical because of the taboo against such criticism. Our compliance to this taboo is an error in judgment that we continue to make. For example, how it is that George W. Bush was not seriously derided when he declared that God told him to invade Iraq? This is an outrageous and very dangerous statement from anyone, never mind that this was coming from the President of the most powerful nation on Earth. It is discouraging that few pundits took issue with his statement. One brave soul who did speak out against Bush's claim to be responding to God's message was Richard Dawkins, the noted biologist, who said, "It is a pity that God didn't vouchsafe him a revelation that there were no weapons of mass destruction."[10]

It is ironic that many religious people who tout themselves as being tolerant and non-judgmental are in fact are among the most intolerant and judgmental of people. Their lack of tolerance feeds toxic exchanges and only furthers our separation from each other. The great scientist and philosopher Carl Sagan lends some historical perspective to this point:

> "The Romans called the Christians atheists. Why? Well, the Christians had a god of sorts, but it wasn't the real god. They didn't believe in the divinity of apotheosized emperors or Olympian gods. They had a peculiar, different kind of god. So it was very easy to call people who believed in a different kind of god, atheists. And that general sense that an atheist is anybody who doesn't believe exactly as I do prevails in our own time."[9]

---

9   Christopher Hitchens, *God is not Great: How Religion Poisons Everything.* New York: Twelve, Hatchette Book Group, 2007). Harris, *Christian Nation*, 79–83.

10   Dawkins, *God Delusion*, 112.

In his book *God without Religion*, Sankara Saranan comments about a discovery he made in his writing: "I concluded that anyone advocating unquestioning loyalty to a restrictive group such as a faith, a territory, or nation was in fact promoting the fall of humanity by promoting its division."[10]

Many religions have kept alive the hateful memories of the enemies who long ago killed, raped, plundered, and otherwise abused and insulted the dignity of their ancestors. These hateful memories get recalled regularly in their cultures to trigger the desire among the younger generation of warriors to even the score for the atrocities perpetrated in wars that happened centuries ago. With their testosterone fired up for revenge toward these historical enemies from different nations and religions, these young warriors are ready to fight for the honor of their ancestors. This multi-generational hostility that is rooted in past injustices needs to stop now. Peace will not be moved forward by cycles of retribution. Religions that promote such intolerance need to replace these ancient and worn out ways with a new set of beliefs where tolerance and understanding prevail. The Christian premises of "love thy neighbor" and "thou shalt not kill" are too often contradicted by their own history of abuse, bigotry, and war. Such hypocrisies are huge obstacles to religion's efforts to contribute to global peace.

History reveals that the majority of followers in the three major religions have been locked into a pattern of passivity by accepting their doctrines without question. In today's Information Age, we are slowly awakening and beginning to question our patterns of passivity. Even in the United States, we have often been blinded by the subtle but powerful influence that religion has had on such things as our patriotism. For example, when I was a boy, the old hymn "Onward Christian Soldiers," made me feel proud, strong, and even heroic to be an American. I pictured my Uncles fighting against the Germans and the Japanese during World War II, as they went "marching as to war, with the cross of Jesus, going on before." In today's more complicated global issues, these destructive delusions about solving conflicts by going to war with other cultures and their religions are much less likely to be seen as 'politically correct'. On one hand we are taught to be more multicultural aware and tolerant of the messages from the traditions of other faiths, and on the other hand, we still want to see dictatorships brought down with the hope that democracy will set them free and create stability and cooperation with other nations.

The major religions of the world today still exert inordinate influence in the particularly painful passage of nations, as they try to resolve their own inherent contradictions to justice.

The Road Being Less Traveled

Attendance has greatly diminished in Christian churches in the United States and in Europe. We know that if religions do not become more relevant they will continue to see the number of people at their services declining. In an article called *Keeping the Faith*, Russell Shorto reports that in Western Europe as a whole, fewer than 20 percent of people (Catholic or Protestant) say they go to church twice a month or more, noting also that in England fewer than 8 percent go to church on Sundays. In some countries that figure is below 5 percent.[11] Sociologists and even some church officials routinely apply the term "Post-Christian" to Europe and parts thereof. We might conclude that Europeans feel that Christianity no longer carries the power of relevance, and stability, and can in fact be a dangerous and misleading road. In a recent survey by researchers at the University of Wales, it was found that only 60 percent of the Church of England's clergy believe in the virgin birth, and 1 in 33 doubt the existence of God![12]

In the United States, a survey by the Institute for Human Studies found "an estimated 14 percent of Americans profess to have no religion, and among 18 to 25 year olds, the proportion rises to 20 percent." The Pluralism Project at Harvard validates this alarming exodus, telling us "nearly 40 million people in the United States have no religious affiliation. That's up to almost 15 percent of the population, from less than 10 percent in 1990."

We are living in a time when the brotherhood and sisterhood of all human beings shouts in our faces for the need to acknowledge our common bonds and to get on with building a world that serves the well being of all. The recent *National Geographic* program on public television that traced

---

[11]   Russell Shorto, "Keeping the Faith," *New York Times Magazine* (April 5, 2007), 42 and 43.

[12]   Ibid.

the origins and migration of early humans through DNA samples from people of all races from all corners of the Earth revealed that there are no fundamental differences in the DNA of humans. Skin color, hair, and structural differences may be accounted for by evolutionary adaptations made according to the environments in which these exterior differences emerged.

Even though we have yielded to religions' claim of authority in our spiritual life for centuries, we know in our hearts that no institution can contain or define the magnificence of this natural creative force some of us choose to call God. We are awakening from our multi-millennia stupor to realize that the path we have taken in following our religions without question, no longer serves us well.

CHAPTER FIVE

God Is Not A Human Figure

All major religions portray God as an all-powerful being who presides over all things. We are told that He abides in heaven and is full of wisdom, that He sees everything, knows everything. And we are led to believe that he gives favors to people who behave in the right ways and especially to those who make the effort to prove that they have total faith in Him.

He, Him, His

And so, those of us who live within the Western Judeo-Christian traditions have learned that when we think of God, we picture a *Him*, a male human figure. *He* is an older Caucasian man with a white beard, long white hair and wearing a white a robe. We refer to everything in the natural world as *His* kingdom. We offer our prayers to *Him*, and when we speak of God, we speak of *Him* and *His* domain. We have been conditioned to see *Him* as our benevolent and all-powerful *Father*, and here on Earth all living creatures are *His* family. *He* represents the ultimate goodness and righteousness, and as such, we thank *Him* for our good fortune and feel obliged to follow *His* ways.

One might wonder, is God a man or a woman, old or young, African or Asian, Hispanic or Caucasian, or a Middle Eastern blend? We might also wonder, can there be such a God in human form? The faithful of the three major religions believe that their God has chosen their religion to be the right one out of the more than one hundred religions on Earth? Most difficult to imagine of all is that some human form of God could have the power to create the stars, planets, moons, galaxies, black holes, and all the wonders of the universe. In every rational way, at the core of our being, we know that a flesh and blood biological being could not have designed or created the universe. We really do know better!

In spite of knowing better, we remain blindly loyal to these beliefs to which our minds have been conditioned. We have gone along with our religions stories to honor our parents, grandparents, and on through many greats of great-grandparents in our ancestral pool, back some thousands of years. This loyalty is mixed with issues of our unexamined pride, along with our passivity and compliance that we masquerade as faith.

The Washing of the Brain

Since childhood, we have been deeply conditioned to accept the liturgies created by our religions. We learned to pray to God as all powerful and all seeing Father, an omnipotent judge who could intervene at any time, with any person, and in any situation. Rabbi David Cooper writes, "As long as we relate to God as Father and we as children, we sustain the dysfunctional paternalistic model in which Father knows best. We not only remain alienated with a sense of abandonment, we relinquish our personal sense of responsibility. Thinking this Father will take care of everything."[13]

Our religious cultures have instructed us to try hard to be good and to please Him. We learn to watch our step as guilt and shame remind us of the boundaries of evil and sin. We need to challenge the belief that He is a vengeful God and could and would punish us if we step out of line. For much of our lives, we have endured this conditioning that uses both fear and rewards.

Christopher Hitchens comments on this brain-washing: "If religious instruction were not allowed until the child had attained the age of reason, we would be living in a quite different world."[14] We have to ask ourselves, is this idea we have about God from thousands of years ago the best we can do? Is this the way we want it to be for the next thousand years? Are

---

13 Rabbi David Cooper, *God Is a Verb: Kabbalah and the Practice of Mystical Judaism* (New York: Riverhead, 1997), 73.

14 Hitchens, *God Is not Great*, 220.

we forever bound to these myths and metaphors offered up as literal? I don't think so.

The walls of every major museum in Europe are adorned with hundreds of paintings and sculptured pieces of Jesus. There he is, all cut and bleeding on the cross, or as a baby, sitting on Mary's lap, both with halos. There will likely be several pieces of art showing God and the angels in the heavens. These artifacts reveal their culture from five and six hundred years ago. Their images speak to the dedication and honor they paid to their religious traditions. We see this devotion in their music, as well as in the architecture of their cathedrals and churches. And here we are, all these hundreds of years later, continuing to think that God is some human figure looking as he does in Michelangelo's painting on the ceiling of the Sistine Chapel. Do we really believe that our universe, and all of life on Earth, was created by such a human figure God? Or is this God-as-man simply a metaphor that no one has bothered to look into? The truth is that most of us don't want to think about it and don't bother to think about it. We simply accept that this is the God who created the universe and everything in it about six thousand years ago. And He did it in six days!

A few centuries later, Christians learned from their New Testament scriptures that God created an immaculate conception with Mary for the birth of Jesus Christ. Then the scriptures tell us that God sacrificed Jesus, His only begotten son, after only four years of ministry, and He did this because He so loved the world and because He wanted us to have everlasting life. What kind of a God is this that He would sacrifice His son? How crazy is this? The concept of a God of this sort is very difficult to imagine in this day and age. But on we go, accepting these things as truth, never bothering ourselves to think much about it, because we are reminded over and over again that this is the word of God. Quietly we go along, not challenging any of these doctrines, because to do so would be a sacrilege, placing us on the margins of our own culture and community. Being an outcast is a very serious consequence of such a challenge, because we want more than just about anything to be accepted. Compliance in keeping silent with our doubts is made easier because we don't have to think about God and how everything came to be. This thinking has already been taken care of for us by the ancient religions of our ancestors! We have learned not to question the fantasies and metaphors; taking them, *quite literally*, as they are offered. But in fact we do need to question these things and to think about them! We have been mired in the roots of our religious beliefs far too long.

God Does Not Play Favorites

Teaching children to believe that God will favor us if we are well behaved is a powerful way for us to shape their thoughts, beliefs, and behavior. Over time this fantasy brings us to believe that God is on our side in wars, and also that He favors our sports teams. It doesn't matter if our opponents also think God is on their side; *we still believe and trust that our God will favor us,* favor our nation, our family, and our team.

Making God an intentional entity creates strange ironies. Did the holocaust happen for a "divine" reason? Why did God make the Black Death or the Great Irish Potato Famine? Christians make no bones about asking God for favors, and if any of their wishes come true, they thank God and praise Him to the skies. Even if two hundred thousand people die in a tsunami, there will be survivors who still thank God for allowing them to live another day. Does that mean that those who died were sinners? They did not believe in their God with enough conviction? Did they not pray enough? If one of our own family members survives an automobile crash, even though four others perish, we thank God! What kind of a God is this that we are thanking?

If we lose someone in a tragic accident or to an illness, we have clichés like "It was just her time to go" and "God must have needed him more than we do," or we might say "she is in a better place now." We tell these awful lies to ourselves as we seek comfort and somehow we feel obliged to forgive God so that we might avoid His wrath.

Einstein was very clear about the position of science is these matters, writing: "There was one religious concept that science could not accept; a deity who could meddle at whim in the events of his creation."[15] He reminded us that that our fate is not determined by some God rolling the dice.

---

15 Walter Isaacson, "Einstein and Faith," excerpted in *Time* magazine (April 16, 2007), 48.

But a Natural God that is a force and *not a being* will not make such judgments, There will be no favor given to one tribe of people over another, nor any consideration given for dealing out retribution or threat to any person. Accepting a Natural God will reduce the confusion surrounding the myths and miracles of the religious stories. We will stop deluding ourselves about the myths and messages the God of our religious tradition sends us. We will cease to blindly believe that God is doing the right thing, and that we should be acting according to his will. This notion of a God of intention distorts our rational thought, as it feeds superstitions into our reality. We need to claim our rational thoughts and challenge these mindless sayings as we engage in a civil discourse on all these issues. One can be certain that we will be labeled as blasphemous if we challenge the efficacy of religions mythological traditions regarding the history of the genesis of humans. We will also be judged as sinners, and condemned as heretics. The consequences of challenging these sacred scriptures can be devastating, which makes it very difficult, if not impossible, to speak or write in opposition to these ideas. Even with our constitutionally guaranteed freedoms of assembly, press, speech, and religion we are too timid to defy these time encrusted cultural norms. Given all that judgment, It is most important to remember that we are free, and may choose not to follow any religion. We are also free to choose not to feel guilty about it.

Religious followers continue to assume that their faith will take care of all matters of their soul, even if their affiliation with religion is casual, shallow, and informal. Regardless of the depth of their commitment to religion, many people continue to delude themselves by believing that their spiritual life belongs to their religion. For those not claiming and owning their individual spirituality, their lives will remain largely unexamined and untapped for the wisdom of their soul within. Yielding to the protocols of our religious institutions, we *fail* to take responsibility for considering our spirituality as being the most important dimension of our human experience.

Giving Up Our Deference

It is time to let go of our deference to the traditions of our religions. We need to stop complying with the doctrines, myths, metaphors, and stories that are frozen in time. We owe it to ourselves to challenge anything that does not make sense to us. Many of our archaic religious traditions not only don't serve us well, they hone the competitive interface with other religions, and thus contribute to being a root cause of wars.

When we accept that we are stuck in the false assumptions of our religious traditions, we will break the chains of long locked doors and open ourselves to the possibilities and opportunities for defining and clarifying our own beliefs about what our spiritual life is and can be.

Challenging and changing our own enmeshment with these engrained patterns, so predictably passed along in our culture, will require a major shift in our consciousness regarding our beliefs. These cultural patterns are highly polarized and politicized, and there will be great resistance to any changes we attempt to make in the status quo. Abandoning our deference to religions dominance will place us in hostile opposition to those loyal to their churches, temples, and mosques. Our challenges and our refusal to conform will be discounted, and we will be called heretics, pagans, infidels, atheists, and the like. This resistance has rendered us afraid to challenge our doubts as we adhere to the biblical metaphor of being the sheep in the Shepherd's flock ("The Lord is my Shepherd I shall not want" from Psalms 23). This poignant image resonates with the truth of our meekness and only underscores our avoidance of searching within for meaning. Conventional wisdom has long told us that our "best citizens" are God-fearing people, and for too long, we have accepted this threat as true. We need to be finished with our deference to religion. Dawkins reminds us of the dangers of giving mammals God-like authority: "To the vast majority of believers around the world, religion all too closely resembles what you hear from the likes of Robertson, Falwell, or Haggard, Osama Bin Laden or the Ayatollah Khomeni. These are not straw men, they are all too influential, and everybody in the modern world has to deal with them." [16]

---

[16] Dawkins, *God Delusion*, 15.

How is it that these self-appointed messengers get off being so arrogant? Sam Harris hits the nail on the head when he writes: "There is, in fact, no worldview more reprehensible in its arrogance than that of a religious believer; the creator of the universe takes an interest in me, approves of me, loves me and will reward me after death; my current beliefs, drawn from scripture, will remain the best statement of the truth until the end of the world; everyone who disagrees with me will spend eternity in hell."[17]

---

[17]   Harris, *Christian Nation*, 74.

CHAPTER SIX

Not Who, But What Is God?

Man is manifestly not the measure of all things. This universe is shot through with mystery. The very fact of its being, and of our own, is a mystery absolute and the only miracle worthy of the name.
—Sam Harris[18]

When religions give this mystery of creation a name, such as God, Allah, Yahweh, or whatever, the mystery appears to be greatly reduced. Just because we have a name for this Supreme Being, we think we understand it. Followers of the major religions embrace the idea that this Supreme Being, a humanlike male who speaks the same language as we do, hears our giving of thanks and praise, and answers our prayers. Religious stories are handed down as the absolute truth with great certainty. They actually *downplay the mystery* of the universe and of life itself, reminding us that if we don't understand, we should have faith. So now that we have faith, there is no mystery—Yahweh, God, or Allah will take care of everything.

Religions do not entertain the idea that God is a force within all life; their emphasis is on an outside God who is omnipotent and is residing in heaven. Each has claimed that if you want to know the truth about God, you should read their scriptures. Never has any publication been less read and so highly esteemed by such a large number of unthinking followers.

In all fairness, we need to remember that the authors of these scriptures were men who were touted as infallible, but alas, were as fallible as we are. These writers were no less locked into the culture of their time than we are by ours. We are long past due in dismissing the idea that God is

---

[18] Sam Harris, *The End of Faith: Religion, Terror, and the Future of Reason* (New York: W. W. Norton, 2004), 47.

humanlike in form. It is a lie to tell us that God is a He or a She with an ageless biological body dwelling in the heavens above.

Accepting the idea that God is not a 'who' does not mean that there is no God. But if God is not a *who*, then *what* is God? Atheism is not the only default position! Since we all came from somewhere, we should, in our search for meaning, consider that there must be an incomprehensible, ubiquitous, and inexplicable Natural Force that created this unknowable and magnificent mystery we call life. Einstein[19] had this to say about mystery:

> "The most beautiful emotion we can experience is the mysterious. It is the fundamental emotion that stands at the cradle of all true art and science. He to whom this emotion is a stranger, who can no longer wonder and stand rapt in awe, is as good as dead, a snuffed-out candle."

Einstein reminds us that it is arrogant to think that we must know everything about everything. Mystery is a reality, and as such, keeps us grounded, and gives us a proper perspective of humility. We should accept the mystery of this Creative Force with all humility and gratitude.

> *There is an undefinable God that pervades everything.*
> —Mahatma Gandhi

While none of us are able to define God with any sense of fully knowing, it is important to acknowledge that we all need to come to terms with our own concept of God. Here is my attempt:

> *God is a mystery that I accept as the Natural Force that created the universe and all life on earth. In that sense, we are all of God and thus capable of expressing something of this Force that is within us. The main thing we can do here on Earth with this Force within us is to serve all life in the interest of the common good.*

---

[19] Albert Einstein, *Time* magazine (April 16, 2007), 47.

By accepting the idea of a magnificent creative Force and leaving the *who* question out of the formula, we create a wider lens to consider the questions of *what* is God? What is this Force other than a mystery? What is it in this Force that wants to create life that continually adapts in ways that are in the best interests of the individual organism, and also in the best interests of the species? Might we assume that the ultimate adaptations of every species are in the best interests of the balance that exists between all life forms?

Spirit and Evolution

It is reasonable to assume that since we are *of* this Force, it must be within our DNA, the blueprint of our cellular structure. Over millions of years, adaptations are assimilated into our DNA a development that enhances the advantages for each individual organism, ultimately enhancing the whole species. These assimilations happen on an unconscious level, the exception being that as the human brain has expanded and evolved, we have become aware that this particular adaptation opens doors to our consciousness and a better understanding of what is going on in our lives. This evolution of our human brain includes our cognitive array of logic, perception, analysis, and memory, as well as the integration of all of these into our consciousness. It is our consciousness that is the source of our decision-making process and includes the commitment to follow our choices with purposeful action. Like the sun coming up every morning, our evolving consciousness dawns on us, enabling us to see that we are human beings on a small planet in a vast universe, reasonably capable of coping with life's challenges and getting better as we go along. We may think of this consciousness as our *soul* as we move toward becoming more grounded in awareness of our *self* in relationship with all of our life's experiences.

Consciousness is the core of our spiritual life. It is our soul "self" that makes us capable of doing much to improve our lot in life, as we positively interact with other humans and other life forms with whom we share the resources of the planet. Consciousness is our interface with the Force of God within and is the vitality that motivates us to work for the common good. This idea of a Creative Force of God within is quite different from what religions have taught us.

The great theologian and philosopher Paul Tillich considered God as our "Ground of Being." This most important theme of Tillich's work is beautifully summarized by Jared Kass: "Tillich suggested our inability to experience God's presence was a result of the traditional conceptualization of God as separate from humanity. Tillich proposed a different conceptualization of God as: 'The Ground of Being', the in-dwelling foundation of existence, the spiritual essence. As the spiritual essence "within" the person, God could be an experienced reality; and the knowledge of our relationship with the Ground of Being could provide an essential element in the resolution of our ultimate concerns."

After reading the letters of Mother Teresa expressing her angst about not feeling God's presence for many years, I wonder if her despair was a result of her seeing "God as separate from humanity," as Paul Tillich described.[20]

Rabbi David Cooper suggests, "The closest we can come to thinking about God is as a process rather than a being."[21] Cooper sees God as a verb, not a noun. It makes sense that if we think of God as a process, we may have deeper appreciation for evolution and the accompanying DNA adaptations. Since everything that is alive is constantly adapting, we can appreciate that evolution is the most pervasive creative process within all of life. Darwin has shown us that, if conditions are favorable, the force within all life moves in a positive direction, always adapting and evolving. Karen Horney brings this down to earth, reminding us with backyard practicality, "You don't have to teach an acorn how to be an oak tree; all it needs are the right conditions."[22]

---

[20] Jared Kass published this paper on Paul Tillich in the *Journal of the American Counseling Association,* April 22, 1991. The title of the article is: Integrating Spirituality into Personality Theory and Counseling Practice.

[21] David Cooper, God Is a Verb, 69.

[22] Clark Moustakes, *The Self* (New York: Harper and Rowe, 1956), 39.

Since this adaptive life force is a growth-oriented phenomenon, we can reasonably assume that the overwhelming predilection of human life is to be good to each other, to collaborate, cooperate, and to support each other as we move in the direction of fulfilling our potential.

Tangible Human Spirit

The dictionary tells us that *spirit is our animating principle*. It is the breath of life. It is the source of our vitality, our aliveness. It is our zest for life! These tangible acts allow us to observe ourselves in our daily lives. We see ourselves in our attitudes, our choices, and our behaviors. Think back and remember times in your own lives when you have had unusual vitality, with enthusiasm, warmth, humor, and the capacity to be fully present and aware of yourself and others in the moments of your experiences. These qualities come from our inner spirit. These are the qualities we express when we feel most authentic and most passionate about life. When we are touched by the generosity and kindness of another person, our feelings of aliveness are greatly enhanced, and the vitality of our spirit is lifted. As our consciousness expands, we become more capable of manifesting our sprit, choosing it, and claiming it as the essence of who we are. We need to honor this aliveness as *the essence of our being*. Brian Thorne is a colleague in England who has authored several books on spirituality, and I especially like the way he put it:

> "My spirit and your spirit are what ultimately define us: it is our spirit that gives meaning and direction to our experience, it is our spirit that determines our identity and it is our spirit which bears the mark of mortality.
> We are body mind and spirit but it is the spirit that breathes life and gives light—or colludes, with death and darkness. The existentialists' question:
> 'who am I?' can only be satisfactorily answered in terms of the spirit."[23]

---

[23]   Brian Thorne, *Person Centered Counseling and Christian Spirituality: The Secular and the Holy* (London: Whurr Publishers, 1998).

If our spirit is ultimately how we are known, it is our responsibility to develop this dimension of our inner life as we clarify our values and beliefs. This is a process of asking ourselves difficult questions about who we are and how we want to be. We understand that we are whole human beings, but we also need to understand that it is our spirit consciousness that mediates this wholeness of self as we perceive and experience our intellect, our memory, our emotions, and our intuitive wisdom. As our spirit integrates and brings balance to our lives, we come to trust it and allow it to guide us.

It is our consciousness that seeks balance between our purposes and our enjoyment of life as we move on our path of discovery. It is good to be social, to be sexual, to be playful, and to enjoy life, but we have other callings if we are to fulfill our potential. We must listen to the wisdom of our inner voice as we ask, "Are there things I should be doing to fulfill my creative self as I serve others? What do I want to do with my life? Marianne Williamson in her book, *A Return to Love*, reminds us of the importance of our asking these questions when she writes:

> Our deepest fear is not that we are inadequate.
> Our deepest fear is that we are powerful beyond measure.
> It is our Light, not our Darkness, that most frightens us.
> We ask ourselves, who am I to be brilliant, gorgeous, talented fabulous?
> Actually, who are you NOT to be?
> You are a child of God. Your playing small does not serve the world
> There is nothing enlightened about shrinking so that other people won't feel insecure around you.
> We were born to make manifest the glory of God that is within us.
> It's not just in some of us; it is in everyone.
> And as we let our Light shine, we unconsciously give other people permission to do the same.
> As we are liberated from our own fear, our Presence automatically liberates others.[24]

---

[24] Marianne Williamson, *A Return to Love* (New York, Riverhead Books, 2012).

This rings very true for me, but I know personally that it is not always easy to claim our strengths, our beauty, and our talents. As children, various injunctions are often presented that are oppositional to the idea of self-affirmation. For example, here are some things I heard from a parent, an aunt or uncle, a teacher, or a grandparent when I was growing up:

- "Don't toot your own horn."
- "Who do you think you are?"
- "You are getting too big for your britches!"

These injunctions impinge upon us in more subtle ways as well. I am remembering an old hymn called "Jesus Loves Me" from my boyhood days in Sunday school and church. Part of the lyric of that hymn goes like this: "We are weak and he is strong." While there is no reason to doubt that Jesus was strong in many ways, this well-meaning old hymn subtly indoctrinates us away from seeing that God is a life Force within all, and that we are not weak—we too are strong! We must override these direct and indirect messages, claim our strength within, and take responsibility for choosing our best ways in life. This will be our way for answering the questions: Who am I? What will I become? Who do I choose to be?

Bailing Out of False Beliefs

Until we *let go* of our culturally indoctrinated belief systems and worn out injunctions, we won't discover that the true Force of our lives comes from within and that it is pointless to ask for favors from an outside God. We are given a finite life and the freedom to make our own choices to create of this life what we can. Letting go of *God as the Father* will be easier when we see and accept that all of the choices we make are our own responsibility.

CHAPTER SEVEN

Soul, The Source Within

Soul is the core of our consciousness, the source of our vitality and our decision maker in every aspect of our life. And yet, in spite of the huge importance of that claim, in most cultures there is an unspoken taboo against talking about our soul, particularly if that conversation is about our soul as being separate from religion. Religion is such a dominant voice in our culture that we are highly reluctant to challenge any norms that keep this social convention on safe ground. We have learned to respect the privacy of others and not to tread on another person's religious beliefs.

The Reticence We Have for Claiming Our "Soul"

To discuss soul issues apart from religion is to border on heresy. If we initiate soul discussions with others, we fear we might be judged, either as invasive or as being too forward about our point of view. Others may think we are weird, or too serious. We fear they may gossip about us or put us down to others. Our reputation could be damaged because our ideas are not in alignment with the mainstream of our culture. Sensing this, we remain guarded and unwilling to open up this topic for discussion. Most of us don't want to talk about our soul, because it's too personal and perhaps too egocentric. Our inner monitor often tells us, "Just be quiet and comply to the norms. Others don't want to hear about your soul." In our compliance to these norms we avoid soul-searching conversations.

We rationalize our failure to challenge the hold that religions have on these well-established norms concerning our soul, by telling ourselves, "Let the academics in psychology, philosophy, anthropology, and sociology speak out against this, or let the religious scholars, clerics, and theologians do the challenging. After all, these are the experts and this is their domain." The problem with this deference is that we don't consider that most of these so-called experts are just as trapped as we are by the boundaries of their own professional norms when it comes to challenging religious doctrine. I am a good example of this reticence to challenge these norms. As a professor of Counseling Psychology for forty-two years, I never heard the mention of soul in any classroom or conference, nor did I see the word soul in textbooks or professional journals. Soul was not a word or an idea to be found in the secular curricula. The irony is that *the word psychology literally means "the study of the soul."* I had somehow repressed this knowledge for nearly thirty of those years. Like the rest of my mainstream colleagues, I was caught up with the notion that soul does not fit in with the mission of establishing and maintaining professional credibility. I did not allow myself to think outside this very well sealed box. But I came to realize later in my career that in our failure to address the idea of soul, we were denying legitimacy of a viable field of inquiry about human experience. Spirituality should not be trashed as "ethereal," because there is much that is tangible and observable in our behavior that is rooted in human spirit. When it comes to taking our soul and our human spirituality seriously, academics have joined with the rest of the culture in being like ostriches with their heads in the sand. The silent injunction for this avoidance is "Leave well enough alone." To explore these issues outside the norm is to risk damaging one's professional standing.

Because psychology is a relatively new profession, the founders of our field tried very hard to establish scientific credibility with academic rigor. Although unspoken, it was clear that ideas about the soul would not gain respectability for psychology among the other disciplines of the academy.

In a similar manner we avoid the topic in social conversation. We find it safer to stay away from discussing considerations of the soul. We focus instead on more comfortable but superficial themes, talking about the weather, food, sports, alcohol, television, computers, and movies, with a bit of latitude allowed for gossiping about relationships. These topics tend to keep us from looking within ourselves to seek answers to more serious questions about our lives.

As we avoid the openness of talking about these more serious matters, we fall into the cramped stereotyped modalities of being skeptical, jaded, or apathetic. We want to give the impression of being cool. Keeping it light makes it easy to take ourselves off the hook of any existential searching. The problem with this avoidance is that many people will not take themselves seriously for a lifetime. It's fine to be lighthearted and not overly intense, but if we are to be fully human, we need to be open in our search for balance and meaning in our lives.

Challenging Cultural Barriers

To reduce the power of these perceived cultural barriers, we need to claim our soul self, our inner human spirit. To do this, I invite you to ask yourself two questions

(1) . . . DO I HAVE A SOUL? AND (2) . . . HOW WOULD I DEFINE MY SOUL?

Take just a couple of minutes to reflect on these questions and write down in a paragraph or so on how you would define your soul. There are no wrong answers.

In a survey I conducted over a span of three years, I put these questions to my graduate students and professional counselors who were participants in my workshops both here in the states, as well as in Ireland and Taiwan. The demographics of the participants were 90 percent women, ranging from twenty-two to fifty years old, with a median age of twenty-seven. I asked them not to put their names on their responses to ensure anonymity, and I made no leading comments or cues as to any specifics the definition might include. They had a blank slate on which to write their responses. Of the more than two hundred respondents, all but one reported that they believed they had a soul. For all the others, I was pleasantly surprised by the thoughtful and personal definitions that participants offered and by the common threads among them. I have included a small sampling below so that you may get the gist of their definitions and common themes. Before you read these, answer the two questions above in order to avoid having your answers overly influenced by the examples below.

Anonymous Definitions of Soul

> *"My soul is the fire that keeps me changing and growing. It is the glow from within that sends me forward and allows me to open up to change."*

> *"Soul is the inner strength that keeps you going through bad times. It is what you use to make tough decisions. It is the good part of yourself that you want to pass on to your children. It is your moral compass that allows you to decide right from wrong."*

> *"Soul is who I am, who I choose to be. What I believe to be true. Soul is the good. My soul is what I leave behind when I'm gone from this world. Soul is my choice maker."*

> *"Soul is the connection between myself and god who is there with me. Soul/spirit guides and watches over the good and bad and brings the best to light."*

> *"Soul is my core being, a part of me that grows and develops despite myself and those around me. My soul is my inner voice, my first teacher."*

I was surprised and also pleased to see that these very personal reflections reveal that most people had indeed given considerable thought to their own souls.

This survey affirmed for me that many others see their souls as their interface with a force that lies within. Believing in this inner force as the source and expression of our soul does not in any way take away from the reverence or the awe in which I stand of the magnificent mystery of our universe, and of life on Earth. Quite the opposite—it makes the idea of a Natural God as a Creative Force come alive. We are all endowed with a very powerful source of vitality from that Force. This is how I would define my own soul today:

My soul is my innermost self and my interface with the Creative Force in the universe that we sometimes call God. It is the deepest part of me that opens my awareness to experience awe and wonder and to be in touch with my feelings of gratitude and humility. My soul is the moral fiber guiding my choices and my purposes of being. It is the seat of my consciousness and the source of my compassion, love, generosity, and kindness.

Ralph Waldo Emerson describes what he calls "Over-Soul":

All goes to show that the soul of man is not an organ, but animates and exercises all organs; is not a function, like the power of memory, of calculation, of comparison, but uses these as hands and feet; is not a faculty, but a light; is not the intellect or the will, but the master of the intellect and the will; is the background of the being, in which they lie,—an immensity not possessed and that cannot be possessed. From within or from behind, a light shines through us upon things, and makes us aware that we are nothing, but the light is all.[25]

Later in that same piece, Emerson closes with, "All reform aims, in someone particular, to let the soul have its way through us; in other words to engage us to obey."

Emerson seems to agree that the source of our vitality comes from a light within. Our job is to choose to turn on the light. Choice is the key that will access the energy of our spirit. As we become more aware, more conscious of this soul self of ours, we understand that this is the essence of our being, that which drives us to live life to the fullest.

Our spirit reveals our whole range of humanness, as we express our laughter, our tears, our willingness to be vulnerable, and to be real. When we truly connect with another, without the social masks of our egos, there

---

[25]   Ralph Waldo Emerson, *"Self Reliance and Other Essays:"* Dover Thrift Editions; (Minola,NY:, 1993).

is trust, respect, and mutuality, a sense of "we." This is the soul stuff of friendships, of mating and of family love.

Spirituality Meaning and Purpose

Love is the nature of the soul.
—John O'Donahue[26]

Here are some down-to-earth ways that I define tangible dimensions of our spirit:

- A sense of meaning and purpose that is rooted in serving others
- The ability to express love and receive love
- The knowledge that the wisdom of our best self is found in our life force within that seeks health, balance and fulfillment
- Inner peace

In our quest for meaning and purpose, we get closer to our own soul, our own essential humanness. We see more clearly that we have an opportunity to create a world where love and compassion for our fellow humans are higher priorities than our greed for material gain.

It is easy to see that compassion, tenderness, warmth, caring, kindness, and gratitude all stem from love and have elements of each other in various mixtures. Our human spirit resonates deeply when we are in such meaningful and intimate relationships. When we experience being accepted, understood, appreciated, and acknowledged in a very personal and genuine way, there is a soul connection. These acts of love—tangible, forceful, peaceful, stimulating, and often illusive—express our spirit in natural and lasting ways. Love is the root of all of our nurturing acts.

It is our soul that resonates when we truly connect with another. When we do allow ourselves to experience these deep and vibrant connections with each other and with the magnificence of the world we live in, we reach our most heightened spiritual moments of gratitude, humility,

---

[26] John O'Donahue, *Anam Cara: Spiritual Wisdom from the Celtic World*: London: Bantam Press, 1997).

reverence, wonder, and joy. These things in life are all around us if we open our hearts to see them and invite them in.

Qualities of compassion, kindness, caring, respect, and gratitude are but a few of the complex expressions of our soul. Many other dimensions of our human spirit are experienced when there is acceptance, loyalty, and honesty in relationships. I very much like what Frances Vaughn says: "The overall quality of one's relationships depends on how willing one is to be open, accepting, and loving rather than fearful, covert and defensive."[27] She also challenges us to see that "if every encounter with another is viewed as an opportunity to heal and extend love, one may learn to heal and be healed in relationships."

And like Emerson, we come to see that our soul is the center of our being. It is the source of our essential character and the basis of how we are known. Our soul is available to each of us as the ultimate source of clarifying our choices about our every attitude, every decision, and every act. Given these pervasive and prominent qualities, it seems a bit odd that any significant discussion of soul has been absent in our culture. We need not be passive in claiming our souls and should instead be open to listen and to trust our inner wisdom.

Soul Consciousness: An Exercise

1. Make a quiet time to look within. Admit that you have feelings, care deeply, and are willing to claim your ability to love.
2. Allow any feelings that you are having, to come to your consciousness. Simply observe them, and welcome them.
3. Allow yourself to feel gratitude, to be thankful and appreciative for all you have, and for all your possibilities.
4. Open yourself to experience wonder at the magnificent mystery of it all.
5. Ask your soul *self* questions, such as, "Who am I?" "What do I need to do to get to where I want to be?"
6. Listen, and wait for answers.

---

[27] Vaughn, F. and Walsh R, *The Inward Arc: Healing in Psychotherapy and Spirituality* (Shambala Press, California 1987).

Our spirituality gives meaning to life itself. It is our union, our sense of oneness with all living things. Our spirit permeates all our human qualities and mediates all our behavior, our thoughts and our feelings. It is this connection that integrates our development as we seek balance and meaning in everything we do. It is the essence of who we are. In May 2000, I wrote the following in my journal:

I am more than my body
My eyes, posture, gait and facial expressions
All portals to my 'soul' reveal my truth

I am more than my thoughts, more than my feelings
More than the sum of my actions
I am a whole being of mind, body, and spirit

And it is my spirit that puts all of me together
To orchestrate my life

As we integrate our feelings, thoughts, and behaviors we connect with the intuitive wisdom of our spiritual center. This is the seat of our valuing, our moral compass, and our decision-making. Most people accept the notion that we are body, mind, and spirit, but I'm always amazed when people talk about this trilogy at what a short shrift the spirit has in this discussion. In the mainstream of our culture, spirit is simply not present, never discussed in any significant way, and if it should be considered in some esoteric corner of the planet, it is most often paired with, and seen as synonymous with, religion. They are not synonymous. Religions are institutions that serve groups of people, while our spirit transcends religion and is manifest in every individual choice we make. It is revealed in the powerful language of our body. Our tone of voice, our welcoming posture, our smile, our eye contact, and our gestures all reveal our spirit well in advance of the content of our spoken message. We think we can hide behind our intellect or our charm, but the light of our soul, or lack of it, manifests the truth. Our bodies do not lie and cannot hide the truth.

Dwight Webb, PhD

The Everyday Authenticity of Our Spirit

If we are truly living in our spirit, all of out expressions of self will be authentic. There will be no deceit. Below are some everyday examples of our spiritual authenticity as we express the transparency of our true selves in relationships. These qualities are how we are known to others, they represent the core of our way of being:

- Affable, approachable, acknowledging
- Caring, courteous, comforting, compassionate
- Dependable, dedicated
- Fair-minded, forgiving, flexible, friendly,
- Generous, grateful, good-natured,
- Hopeful, helpful,
- Inclusive, intimate, interested,
- Kind,
- Loving, lovable
- Optimistic, open,
- Polite,
- Reasonable, respectful, responsible,
- Sharing, sincere, steady, supportive,
- Vulnerable, valuing,
- Warm, welcoming, and willing to try

This quick and brief alphabetical sampling gives a glimpse of the broad range and depth of our spirit. We are all to a greater or lesser extent on a continuum (for example: kind vs. unkind) of these and other qualities that define our innermost self. And we have the ability to move our position on that continuum by changing our attitude and consequent behavior as we engage in soulful decision on questions of how we choose to be. Authenticity is at the heart of our human spirit, and the very core of our being alive and conscious of our true selves.

What is generosity, if not a deeply spiritual gift to enhance the well-being of others? What is kindness toward our fellow humans if not from the heart of our spirit? Truth, honesty, and integrity are choices and acts coming from our human spirit, all expressions of our soul.

Francis Vaughn reminds us not to be trapped by the stereotypes of the business-as-usual syndrome that too often puts our sacred and intimate essence on the back burner when she writes, "A healthy relationship makes it safe to let go of masks and defenses and shows one to be fully present in a free feeling exchange with another person."[28]

When I am playing my banjo or singing and laughing with my sons and my extended family and friends, I resonate with kindred spirits. I experience the wide range of my spirit when I let love in. I feel caring, and I feel cared for.

When I free myself from the distractions of the day and stand quietly in reflection at a sunset or a moon rising over the horizon, I experience peace and amazement at the wonder of it all. We need to acknowledge the spirit within us in our daily lives such as when we connect with another in generous acts of friendship and kindness. When we do allow ourselves to be open to such experiences, we are more able to take in the magnificence of the world we live in.

Not long ago, I received the following e-mail from my son Chris. He sent along this message as a "thought for the day":

Humans are powerful spiritual beings meant to create good on the earth.
This good isn't usually accomplished in bold actions, but in singular acts
of kindness between people. It's the little things that count, because they are
more spontaneous and show who you really are.
—Dannion Brinkley[29]

It is true that the wellspring of our soul may be expressed in "little things" such as the warmth in our smiles and the light from our eyes. Recall a time when your eyes met another person's eyes in such a way that in that moment you knew this could be a friend. This is not just an emotional, sexual, or social phenomenon. Such encounters emerge spontaneously from our spirit and touch the spirit of another. When two people are connected in this way, they are on a compatible and resonating energy frequency. There is between them an immediate mutual sense of trust, open communication, and the possibility of true intimacy and

---

28 Ibid., 183.
29 D. Brinkley, quoted in Tom Razetto's *The Mystic View*, "Near Death Experiences," 2007. www.useyourmagic/tmv.

understanding. The following poem titled *Web* from a friend and colleague in Ireland captures this idea well:

> Glistening and gossamer fine,
> An invisible thread
> Fixed your eyes to mine,
> At opposite ends of a line
> Transcending time
> For an instant
> We were briefly caught
> In the transparent web
> Of each other's
> Soul spinning.
> —Pauline Macey[30]

This connection between our heart and soul is often best expressed through poetry. Science cannot measure our spirit with the exactitude that is required of that discipline, and this is as it should be. The miracle of life itself in all its grandeur, the nuanced blending of the colors at sunset or the sounds of music from all the richness of diverse cultures, all transcend the exactitude of science.

Spiritual dimensions may not be reduced to categories of intellect, logic, or social conditioning. In our essence, we are so much more than these labels. We are not yet perfectly attuned in this world of ours, but we are evolving. I very much like what George Bernard Shaw wrote regarding the courage to live his awareness of the force of God within. In the following piece, one can sense his gratitude for the magnificence of life's possibilities.

> This is the true joy in life, the being used for a purpose recognized by yourself as the mighty one; the being a force of nature instead of a feverish selfish little clod of ailments and grievances complaining that the world will not devote itself to making you happy. I am of the opinion that my life belongs to the whole community and as long as I live it is my

---

[30] Pauline Macey is a counselor in Ireland, a former student, a friend, and a fine poet.

privilege to do for it whatever I can. I want to be thoroughly used up when I die, for the harder I work the more I live. I rejoice in life for its own sake. Life is no "brief candle" to me. It is a sort of splendid torch which I have got hold of for the moment, and I want to make it burn as brightly as possible before handing it on to future generations.

CHAPTER EIGHT

Setbacks To Our Spirit

Social scientists have known for a long time that the first year of a person's life, infancy, is extremely important for their later development. Mothers know this instinctively, because it is embedded in her DNA. But these nurturing impulses, and instincts may be overridden in any caretaker if they have been subjected to abuse, neglect, or if they are in a context where there are toxic conditions such as the influence of mind-altering substances. These are the primary causes of setbacks to the development of a healthy spirit.

For the spiritual and physical health of a child in the first year of life, the primary thing that the child needs to know is that this is a world he or she can depend on and trust. Will the mother answer the infant's cues signaling hunger, a need for a diaper change, a high temperature, or some other discomfort? Will the child be comforted? This bonding with the mother is the foundation for all that follows. It needs to be strong in those early years. This nurturance is the key to all later development and the foundation of the soul.

There are those among us who have been discouraged instead of encouraged, those who have been rejected instead of included, and those who have not received the love, respect and compassion necessary to thrive, and in some case, not enough to survive.

Abuse and Neglect

We are born innocent, with a blank slate, open to receiving love from our caretakers. We are also born with a genetic predisposition for making healthy choices that will help us to create a better life on earth for ourselves and for others. But our outcomes in life will also depend to a great extent on the luck of the draw with regard to the qualities of the wellness of our parents, family, friends, communities, culture, and the opportunities provides therein. These are all significant factors, with a powerful ability to shape the forces effecting our total development, and thus our overall well-being. While our genetic code programs us to be nurturing and moral, this predisposition can be overridden by psychological and/or physical abuse from others, be they parents, siblings, teachers, peers, bullies of any age, or any other threatening person in our lives with an angry, rejecting, intimidating, authoritarian, and controlling personality.

In our lifetime, most of us have experienced at least some events and relationships that turned out to be toxic to our spirit and thus to our development. Toxic experiences are wounds to our soul. In our early years, we are particularly vulnerable, being largely dependent on our caretakers for nurturance and protection. At our best, we are resilient and strong, but we can also be vulnerable to psychological insult by significant others. We know that many children may experience negligence and abuse from family members and other primary caretakers, and that these interactions can have profoundly negative outcomes.

Abusers, by their very acts, reveal deficiencies of their own soul with regard to their lack of ability to give proper nurturance. It is predictable that they themselves have been victims of abuse or neglect, wounded by the toxic impact of their so-called caretakers. Research from the Institute on Family Violence has well documented this repeating cycle between the abuser and their own history as victims of abuse.[31] This knowledge has contributed to our understanding of the depth and the consequences of the wounds inflicted by such abuse. All humans are vulnerable to insult. We experience it most directly as a blow to our sense of self, our souls. Think about any such experiences you may have had, and ask yourself *how you felt when you were teased, put down, rejected, betrayed, left out, disregarded, discouraged, or controlled by a domineering authority figure.* We will all have strong reactions to these experiences, particularly if such abusive treatment comes from a family member, friend, or someone we thought we could trust. Continuing interaction with people who are judgmental, blaming, rejecting, cold, and indifferent is insulting and sure

---

[31]   On this topic, The Institute of Family Violence at the University of New Hampshire is the major source for research information.

to dampen our spirits, often with some permanence. We would be well advised to avoid such relationships.

From an early age, we realize that there is something about being judged and evaluated that we do not like. Even praise is sometimes uncomfortable, because we know that this same person praising and judging us as "good" is also capable of withholding their compliments and could judge us negatively if we don't live up to their expectations.

What happens to our spirit when we don't receive the love that we need? What happens when instead we are met with encounters that are full of anger, blame, danger, and shame? The following list captures some of the normal reactions to such negative encounters.

Outcomes from Lack of Love

- Compliance, conformity
- Discouragement and fear
- Withdrawal, avoidance
- Retaliation, revenge
- Angry aggressive and bossy behavior
- Hateful disdain
- Apathy
- Lack of confidence

It is not easy to stand up to and be assertive with abusive people, especially if they are in a power position over you. When this happens, our natural resilient spirit may be so stifled, so smothered, so crushed that we tend to shut down to protect ourselves. Often the result is that we find a person who is angry, withdrawn, pessimistic and cynical in their views of the world. In the absence of a buoyant spirit, we see instead a jaded, skeptical, and depressed outlook on life. If we don't receive at least occasional love and respect, to nurture some semblance of vitality to our spirit, it is very difficult to be hopeful.

The vitality of our spirit, or the lack of it, will always be revealed by our bodies. It will be read by our posture, the way we carry ourselves, and the way in which we engage or don't with others. When we see a person who doesn't feel worthy, we see their dampened spirit immediately in the downward tilt of their head. When people carry shame, they have difficult maintaining eye contact. Self-doubt can be heard in the voice tone, as well as in the words, as these both reveal the speakers lack of confidence. In reading the body language of a person in distress, we know that their spirit is telling us: "Help me to get out of the pain I am in."

A wounded spirit is a malnourished soul that is aching and crying out for love, acceptance, understanding, and caring. Wounds to a person's soul make it difficult for them to trust and to bond with others, and severely impairs them in terms of their developing. When negative energy affects us, we learn to be tentative, closed, and guarded instead of open, welcoming, and trusting. Reflect back on messages from your family members, your peer group, your teachers, your religious training from your early childhood, and see if you got negative messages that were hurtful.

One of my clients—I'll call her Jean (not her name)—wrote in her journal about the negative outcomes from the diagnostic labels she received when she was hospitalized (clinical depression, borderline personality disorder, and schizophrenia) "Labels impose restrictions, unnecessary restrictions on a person. It seems like just another way to control someone who's already feeling powerless."

On another occasion, Jean wrote a note to me about some feelings she had regarding a person she had recently observed on the street.

The Bag Lady

Dwight—

There's a woman, maybe homeless who I see about once a week as she walks the streets and sidewalks. She walked right in front of my car today and I had the greatest urge to Jump out and talk with her though my guess is she never speaks to anyone. She is extremely thin and always wears a long-sleeved coat. She carries a bag—one of those plastic supermarket ones—and wears a scarf pulled way down over her forehead and eyes. She always looks down and turns her head away from traffic and people. Sometimes she talks to herself. What would I say to her? What would I ask her? Who are you? What is your story? When did you first lower your eyes? Does looking down make your world smaller?

Safer? Do you ever talk to anyone? Who cares about you? What do you think about before you go to sleep? What is in your bag? Whose daughter are you? What is scaring you? What is the terror I see on your face? Have you been loved? When were you last held? What do you fantasize about?

Do you fantasize about being held? About being loved? Do you ever look in the mirror? Are you always alone? Do you get lonely? Do you ache and yearn and despair? Do you wish there was someone who understood the constant pain of your loneliness and fear? Do you wish you were dead? Are you afraid of dying alone and cold and alone? Do you wonder if you'll ever feel the touch of another on your skin? Do you long to be held forever? Are you afraid of food? Do you believe in God? Are you afraid of God? Do you think God is punishing you? Are there scars on your body? Are you ashamed? Do you ever feel dirty? Are you afraid of getting lost and not being found? Does anyone ever tell you "goodnight, sleep well"? Do you ever wish you were someone else? When was the last time you smiled and laughed? When was the last time you cried? Are there any pretty things in your life? Do you have wishes? Are you me? What is your story? Be safe.

Jean's humanity and her empathy for this woman were palpable. I was touched by her heartfelt and searching account. She was able to see this woman and herself so very compassionately, and to simply analyze this as my client projecting her issues onto this woman in the street misses the whole point. What is Jean saying about her own soul? What is she telling me about her struggles and the wounds from her own childhood experiences?

The vitality of the expressions of our soul will be determined by the kinds of life experiences we have had. Ask yourselves:

- Did I receive love?
- Did I experience acceptance?
- Have I been understood, cared about, and acknowledged?
- Have I been kept safe?
- Have I bonded with significant family and friends?

- Have I experienced forgiveness or been given a second chance (maybe even a third chance)?

If we can answer yes to these soul experiences, we will thrive and continue to grow because this is the fuel for our power to care and to have compassion. Our strength and resilience depend on these qualities that nourish our spirit. They not only shape us, but over time they will come to define us.

My friend Jason Holder reminded me that no matter the depth of the wound to the soul, with the right nurturance at the right moment, there is hope as long as there is breath. It is important that we open ourselves to understand the conditions that will effect our spiritual development. As we do this, we turn toward the light.

Below is a brief self-rating scale to determine your own life issues. Since none of us have developed into adulthood unscathed, there may be aspects or patterns in your life that you will want to work on in your own spiritual path toward wholeness.

Self-Rating Scale

	Need to Improve	I'm OK
Anger control		
Anxiety		
Self Doubt		
Depression		
Forgiveness		
Hostility		
Self Respect		
Shame		

Put a check mark where you see yourself at this point in your life, and consider keeping a journal to explore other issues that are of concern. Decide how best you want to work on what you have recorded here. Check back with yourself in six months and see how you are doing.

CHAPTER NINE

Evolution: The Creative Force Of Life

All signs are that amino acids are going to be found throughout the galaxy.
They are apparently obvious building blocks with which to construct life.
—Stephen J. Freeland[32]

How did cellular life come about on Earth after things cooled down? How does the force behind the Big Bang and our consequent universe create the conditions for life to emerge? Is it only random that planet Earth is placed in perfect orbiting balance with sun and moon? Are there two Gods, one that created the universe and the other that somehow created the conditions for life? The mysterious origins of both life and the universe are important existential questions. We are gleaning more information from astrophysicists, chemists, biologists and geneticists and we are beginning to form reasonable hypotheses on these important questions. Our problem is that we can't prove or disprove any such hypothesis, because science cannot replicate the conditions and events of the last fifteen billion years.

The Beginnings of Cellular Life

An article in the *Daily Galaxy* raises an important question: "Is Earth's DNA Unique or a Universal Constant?" Stephen J. Freeland of the NASA Astrobiology Institute at the University of Hawaii offers a beginning glimpse toward a reasonable response. "Life has been using a standard

---

[32] Stephen J. Freeland of the NASA Astrobiology Institute at the University of Hawaii, quoted in *The Daily Galaxy Newsletter* (August 29, 2011), 1.

set of 20 amino acids to build proteins for more than 3 Billion years. It's becoming increasingly clear that many other amino acids were plausible candidates, and although there's been speculation and even assumptions about what life was doing, there's been very little in the way of testable hypotheses."[33] Paul Davies, a leading authority in astrobiology and the director of BEYOND: Center for Fundamental Concepts in Science and co-director of the ASU Cosmology Initiative, writes, "To the best of our knowledge, the original chemicals chosen by known life do not constitute a unique set; other choices could have been made, and maybe were made if life started elsewhere many times."[34] The pool of candidate amino acids from which life drew its twenty were discovered within the Murchison meteorite, which fell in Australia in 1969. It was thought that this meteorite dated from the early solar system and therefore represented a sample of which compounds existed in the solar system and on Earth before life began. Aaron Burton a NASA Postdoctoral Program Fellow who works as an astrochemist at NASA's Goddard Space Flight Center, writes, "Although a number of experiments have shown that unnatural amino acids can be incorporated into the genetic alphabet of organisms, it may never be possible to experimentally simulate sufficient evolutionary time periods to truly compare alternate amino acid alphabets."[35]

Until I hear of something that makes more sense, I will accept these ideas of amino acids as key elements in the origins of cellular life on Earth as a reasonable hypothesis. The question is: Does the interaction of amino acids with other chemicals from random elements ignite the birthing of life's most rudimentary cellular forms? If so, it is also the beginning of the astonishing natural selection process of evolution. Billions of years later, Charles Darwin's discovered this process of evolution through natural selection. It is the idea that all life must adapt in order to procreate and ensure continuation of the species. Daniel Dennett acknowledges the significance of Darwin's profound discovery and contribution to our understanding of life, writing, "If I were to give an award for the single best idea anyone ever had, I'd give it to Darwin, ahead of Newton and Einstein and everyone else. In a single stroke, the idea of evolution by

---

[33]   Ibid., 2.

[34]   Ibid.

[35]   Ibid.

natural selection unifies the realm of life, meaning and purpose with the realm of time, cause and effect, mechanism and physical law."[36]

Creatures that are able to adapt will live to see another day. These species-specific physical adaptations occur in organisms over many generations of natural selection, altering the genetic code in ways that are beneficial for procreation and thus for survival of the species. Darwin observed an interesting example of this when he noticed that the beaks of finches on one island grew bigger than the beaks of finches on a nearby island. He concluded that the different sized beaks facilitated food gathering in the different locations. Genetic adaptations serve organisms in a multitude of ways, for example, avoiding danger, building nests, migrating when the time is right, and nurturing their young. Over time, in successful organisms, adaptation becomes embedded in the genetic code and is passed on to their progeny and to the following generations, ad infinitum. The complexity of these adaptations is astonishing. Dennett helps us understand that more clearly when he reminds us that: "The DNA in your body unsnarled and linked, would stretch to the sun and back several—ten or a hundred—times."[37]

All life continues to evolve through the process of natural selection, and any part of an organism that is challenged will attempt to adapt. For example, the human brain and the emergent constructs that we call our mind or consciousness are continuously challenged to deal with the explosion of technology, the massive amounts of information from the Internet, and the high demand for solutions to serious social and political issues of human rights and equal justice. Although much of this evolution may appear to be random, the continuous sloughing, mutating, and creative adaptations allows organisms to make adjustments that clearly enhance their ability to survive and thrive.

In an article by Thomas Hayden, he quotes a piece from Theodosius Dobshansky's famous essay titled "Nothing in Biology Makes Sense Except in the Light of Evolution," wherein Dobshansky concludes, "Evolution is quite simply the way biology works, the central organizing principle of life on earth."[38] On every front, there are new discoveries by genome scientists

---

[36] Dennett, *Darwin's Dangerous Idea*, 21.

[37] Ibid., 151.

[38] Thomas Hayden refers to Dobshansky's essay in *American Biology Teacher* 36 (1973): 125.

that continue to validate and expand Darwin's theory of evolution. Since these are well-documented truths, we can conclude that it is a mistake to dismiss evolution in the argument of how life came to be. I would argue that evolution is the most plausible example of what we might consider the ongoing force of creation. Call this act of creation God, or of the Creator, or a Higher Power, whatever you call it—it is a sacred act.

Atheism, Biology, and Mystery

Julian Baggini writes in his article "Atheism, a Very Short Introduction", "What most atheists do believe is that although there is only one kind of stuff in the universe, and that is physical, out of this stuff come minds, beauty, emotions, moral values, in short the full gamut of phenomena that give richness to human life."[39] Still, science does not claim to know all the answers to the origins of life on the planet, nor can it explain why the physical and chemical laws are so exact in following precise and predictable outcomes. Given these unknowns and others, I dare say that those who claim to be atheists might consider a more modest stance, admit . . . *There must be a natural force that created everything. There must be some unknown higher power, even if we cannot know the mystery behind it all.* Atheists might agree, if what we call God was rooted in naturalism and not supernaturalism, it cold be considered reasonable.

Daniel Dennett challenges all religions to be open to full examination when he asks: "Wouldn't it be a shame to forego the opportunity for a strengthened, renewed creed, settling instead for a fragile, sickbed faith that you mistakenly supposed must not be disturbed? . . . The only meaning of life worth caring about is one that can withstand our best efforts to examine it."[40]

Sam Harris writes, "Any intellectually honest person will admit that he does not know why the universe exists."[41] This truth stands in sharp contrast to the arrogant righteousness of religions that claim absolute

---

[39]   Julian Baggini, *Atheism: A Very Short Introduction* (Oxford: Oxford Press, 2003).

[40]   Dennett, *Darwin's Dangerous Idea*, 22.

[41]   Harris, *Christian Nation*, 74.

authority in having answers to the mystery. Likewise, this sharply contrasts the arrogant and rigid stance of atheism. Religions get away with comments such as "It's God's plan" or "It's God's work," as if they've had the final word. With all humility, religions need to encourage their followers to integrate the knowledge that is available from the sciences, as well as the social sciences, and cease to resist and negate the truth of evolution. Why not call evolution the work of an omnipotent and natural force of God?

Evolution and Consciousness

Among the human DNA adaptations of evolution, we see the emergence of brain functioning that yields higher consciousness than that found in earlier humans or in any other animal form. This higher consciousness allows us to reflect and create meaning in our lives. We have created art and music to express our deepest spiritual feelings. We have harnessed enormous resources and created technology that has opened us to the heavens as well as to the world of nanomolecular discoveries. The more we learn, the more stunning we find our universe to be, and the more likely it is that we must stand in awe at the magnificence of it all.

Higher levels of consciousness allow us to integrate our existential and spiritual qualities, just as our strength, endurance, and resilience allow us to integrate our physical well-being and performance. Those individuals who are the most evolved will continue to be favored with more success in selecting a mate with similar qualities to join them in the holy act of procreation. This rule of genetically endowed features such as intelligence, and higher-level consciousness, continues as we evolve on every front.

Research by Vaillant has shown that love (genuine compassion) and altruism are part and parcel of the evolutionary scheme of things. These qualities of high-level spiritual consciousness would include honesty, trust, and cooperative behavior, and they play an important role in our opportunities and choices.[42] Over generational time, as our spiritual awareness gains prominence, cultures will shift and people will gain a more clear sense of how and when to let go of fear, mistrust, and the

---

[42]   George Vaillant, *Spiritual Evolution: A Scientific Defense of Faith* (New York: Broadway Books, 2008) 20-21.

need to dominate others. The emergence of higher-level consciousness in humans is an extraordinary example of evolution.

Taking Personal Responsibility

We have gleaned at least a vague awareness of our place in the mystery of our universe. The most important thing we have learned is that we need to take responsibility for ourselves as choice makers on every front. A good example of this is seeing the consequences of our choices in the current threats of global warming, and the need this creates to work together with other nations toward effective solutions. There is no magic or miracle fix; it is up to us to make it work, and this calls on us to reach for our greatest strength from within to meet that challenge.

Since evolution manifests its latent potential within all life, we could say that God's work (i.e., evolution) is ongoing. Why wouldn't a creative force set life up for continuous improvement? One might consider that this ongoing process of evolution is in itself an intelligent design set in motion by an unknowable creative force. Norman Cousins had this to say about the unknowable: "Nothing about the universe is more complex, more resistant to the penetrating powers of systematic thought, more diverse in its manifestations, more elusive its antecedents, more electrifying in its capacities, than human life itself."[43] In humans, we know that each new challenge and consequent adaptation stimulates the development of our consciousness, where new possibilities and imagination germinate.

At Work on an Incomplete Bridge

Intelligent design is the theory used to oppose evolution. Its proponents say that if there is a design, there must be a designer, a supernatural God. According to the three major religions of the world, this designer is a human figure God, and not just a force. He is a being, and according to

---

[43] Norman Cousins, *Head First: The Biology of Hope* (New York: E. P. Dutton, 1989), 119.

the Judeo-Christian tradition he did all the design work in six days, resting on the seventh.

These differences of opinion on how life on Earth was created, hinge on two important questions. First, did this creation happen in six days? Or, as the abundant scientific evidence from the fossil record shows, did it happen very slowly over some four billion years? Secondly, was this creation accomplished by a human figure, or by some unknowable force? If God the designer is a human figure, we might ask, "Who or what then designed this God?" At some point we have to conclude that there is a force that continues to unfold that we don't begin to understand.

The stand religions take on intelligent design rejects evolution and all the accumulated scientific evidence. Their oppositional positions remain stuck in their fixed polarized positions. Those who hold to the intelligent design belief are so accustomed to the image of God as a male being, their minds are closed to the possibility that God is a creative force or a process (such as evolution). The idea of evolution just does not fit with what they have been told. Likewise, science is so dedicated to rationality and testable hypotheses that anything short of exact answers is dismissed as shabby thinking. Neither camp leaves enough room for imagination or consideration that might lead to respect for the other's points of view. Their opposition to each other is so entrenched and so dedicated to being right that their minds remain closed. The differences between those who believe that God takes a human form and those who believe in God as a force boils down to believing either the literal translations of the scriptures or the scientific evidence supporting evolution.

Whichever side one chooses to come down on, we are still left with an enormous mystery. Neither camp explains the genesis of life itself in clear and exact terms. Both sides need to admit the truth that Creation itself is beyond our understanding. None of us knows for certain how it all came to be. In spite of this absence of knowing, most of us can accept that the biology of all life continues to be created by some force. It seems reasonable that both camps might agree that this force could be called God given. Making this leap of faith does not require membership in any religion, but it does require us to expand our definition of God to include the idea of a Creative and Mysterious Force. These two opposing camps could readily find points of agreement if two things happened.

1. The proponents of intelligent design acknowledged that evolution is not anti-God. After all, why wouldn't God as a force create life forms that continuously adapt and develop?
2. The evolutionists accepted the term God or the Force of God as a label to explain the mystery behind the cellular adaptation of natural selection? It is not necessary to be an atheist just because you believe in evolution. I dare say that most scientists are not atheists.

Rabbi David Cooper supports the idea of a synthesis between evolution and religion when he writes . . ."Creation is not something that happened at some point in time; creation is happening at all times."[44] Within the biology of our brain, our minds long ago evolved to make us aware of ourselves as both autonomous beings as well as team players who can work in harmony with peers of our tribe to create outcomes that could not be done without cooperation. This idea of team play is supported in Robert Wright's book, *Non-Zero: The Logic of Human Destiny*, in which he points out, "Our genes may be viewed as players, and the rules include an ultimatum: Cooperate to sustain your vehicle or perish."[45] In non-zero sum, the idea is either win-win or lose-lose. If it's win-lose, it's a zero sum game, where one cancels out the other. Win-win is self-generating—the more win-win outcomes, the stronger the species.

Clearly we are coming to higher levels of awareness, and as we do, we become able to break the chains that have bound us to ignorance, prejudice, superstitions, and other forms of narrow-minded conditioning from well-meaning but ill-informed caretakers. Intelligence and awareness (they should not be seen as one and the same, although they do complement each other) will serve us in overriding our mistaken assumptions. We do know that it is in our best interest to make choices that are for the common good, because survival favors such choices.

Every gain in consciousness becomes embedded in the DNA of every cell in our body, and the wisdom within this cellular structure endows each of us to more effectively adapt in the ongoing process of our own creation.

---

[44] Cooper, *God Is a Verb: Kabbalah and the Practice of Mystical Judaism* (New York: Riverhead Books, 1997), 60.

[45] R. Wright, *Non Zero: The Logic of Human Destiny* (New York: Pantheon Books, 2000).

Stuart Kaufman, the author of *Reinventing the Sacred*, thinks it is "a force worthy of being called God" and says that we need to naturalize our deity in this way. God, he points out, "is our chosen name for the ceaseless creativity in the natural universe, biosphere, and human culture."[46] This God is a pervasive force, and we have the choice to accept the mystery of that force with openness of spirit. Kaufman contends that this creative process of emergence "is so stunning, so overwhelming, so worthy of awe, gratitude, and respect, that it is God enough for many of us. God, a fully natural God, is the very creativity in the universe."

In addition to the incredibly diverse life forms on our planet, might there also be a force that has arranged our moon to be in perfect orbit around our planet, placing both these spheres in a precise annual dance around our sun? These outcomes follow exact laws throughout the universe and Daniel Dennett puts these exquisite laws of nature into stunning perspective in the following piece.

> The speed of light is approximately 186,000 miles per second. What would happen if it were only 185,000 miles per second, or 187,000 miles per second? Would that change much of anything? What if the force of gravity were 1 percent more or less than it is? The fundamental constants of physics—the speed of light, the constant of gravitational attraction, the weak and strong forces of subatomic interaction, Planck's constant—have values that of course permit the actual development of the universe as we know it to have happened. But it turns out that if in imagination we change any of these values by just the tiniest amount, we thereby posit a universe in which none of this could have happened, and indeed in which apparently nothing life-like could ever have emerged: no planets, no atmospheres, no solids at all, no elements except hydrogen and helium, or maybe not even that—just some boring plasma of hot, un-differentiated stuff, or an equally boring nothingness. So isn't it a wonderful fact that the laws are just right for us to exist? Indeed one might want to add, we almost didn't make it!

---

46   Stuart Kaufman, *Reinventing the Sacred* (New York: Basic Books, 2008), 129.

And to think, all of this precise unfolding is happening without guidance or prayers from the supernatural views of the religious. As our consciousness evolves, we will more and more bond with the truths of science and will continue to transcend the dogma of religions even as we become more spiritual.

Most of us are beginning to realize and to accept that we are spiritual beings. Our laughter, tears, humor, motivation to cooperate, and the bonds with friendships, family, and community all point to our social/spiritual evolution. These qualities are, in fact, among the most important features of our lives. It is our spirit that defines who we are: courageous, thoughtful, and kind, for example, or their opposites on a continuum. Thankfully, we are moving in a progressive direction on this continuum ever so slowly, yet ever gaining momentum.

If adaptations are working correctly, each new generation should be blessed with the benefits of evolved intelligence, physical strength, good health, beauty, and imagination. In theory we should also be more evolved socially and spiritually as well as physically. I like to think that my progeny and theirs are an evolutionary leap forward in all these dimensions as we all move forward from clumsier times. The emergence of our spiritual consciousness means we are moving toward a greater capacity and ability to love. This ultimately means cooperative effort by all in creating the qualities necessary for healthy and sustainable life on our planet.

Dennett again reminds us, "When comparing the time scales of genetic and cultural evolution, it is useful to bear in mind that we today, every one of us, can easily understand many ideas that were simply unthinkable by the geniuses in our own grandparents' generation!"[47]

---

[47] D.Dennet, *Darwins Dangerous Idea* (New York, Simon and Shuster, 1995), 377.

79

CHAPTER TEN

Morality: Nature And Nurture

Man is here for the sake of other men—above all for those upon whose smiles and well-being our own happiness depends.
—Albert Einstein

Morality is a good example of how nature and nurture are not in an either/or relationship. Instead, they are complementary, working together for the benefit for the organism. With this convergence, morality becomes the voice of our human spirit and the foundation for the well-developed core of our being, our soul. With our mammalian nature, we are wired to be moral and altruistic because it favors survival in a variety of ways, including procreation. Our culture institutions complement this instinct, urging us in all our social development to do the right thing. Because moral issues are not always precisely defined, our instincts need to be guided by our interpretation of the unique and nuanced individual circumstances of the cultures within which we work.

We are biologically programmed to take care of our own young, as well as other members of our own family and community. But if a person is to emerge with full moral functioning and development, there must be additional layers of socialization involved. We must be given certain life lessons on moral behavior, and a deep understanding of the consequences for immoral behavior. If we are to succeed in creating a lasting peace on Earth, individuals must accomplish the synthesis of our biological propensity to be moral in respectful harmony with the norms of other cultures. Religions are particularly stubborn regarding their claim that their way is the only true path to God, and unless we transcend these rigid beliefs, there will be no peace on Earth. Religions must be more accepting, and respectful of the multitude of other diverse cultures with their beliefs, ideologies, and traditions. Human rights will be the foundation upon which global morality rests. No civilized culture can survive indefinitely in a global economy if it is not able to cooperate across borders and cultures in order to secure the rights of all people. Morality with tolerance, and justice will rule the path to peace.

Cultural Influence and Morality

As religions gained more power through the centuries and thus more control within their respective cultures, they claimed the right to defining moral behavior. Morality has become a major part of their curricula. Christians for example, are instructed to follow the Golden Rule, the Ten Commandments, and other doctrines that might be deemed as necessary for the life of a good Christian. Such doctrines would have us believe that Christianity is the rock on which morality stands. The faithful are told that if they believe in Jesus and repent their sins, they will be saved and have everlasting life. Most have accepted these edicts as the gospel truth. In more recent times we have begun to uncover much hypocrisy and irony in their claims of moral infallibility. For example, consider the following events in Christian history, in which a lack of morality among religious leaders was the norm in their historical time and in the context of their culture.

- The Crusades
- The Spanish Inquisition
- Continuing wars of retribution and ethnic cleansing
- Sex scandals involving pedophile priests.

The three major religions have moral rules for obeying and punishments for infractions if any of their flock strays off their path. But In the case within the Catholic Church, they have taken considerable latitude in defining morality when dealing with the immoral behavior of their priests who have committed pederasty (sexual behavior between a man and a boy). This abusive behavior has been tolerated and ignored by the administrative hierarchy from the Pope on down. The Catholic hierarchy has tried to keep these criminal acts a secret, and when called out to answer for these heinous crimes, they typically avoided legal proceedings by offering huge amounts of money to the victims and their families in order to settle out of court. Priests have molested and sexually abused thousands of children over many generations, and the Catholic Church cover-up, is another whole layer of criminal behavior. Any other citizens not so sheltered by the privileged status of their religion would be put in prison in total shame and disgrace for such offenses. Most of the priests who are guilty of these crimes go free and are given a new assignment in another community, only to repeat this abhorrent behavior.

Interestingly and hypocritically, Catholic doctrines use guilt and shame to get followers to conform to their moral codes. They offer the reward of heaven to reinforce and sustain this "proper" behavior among constituents. But with their criminal priests, they look the other way and pretend that a crime never happened. The radical warring wing of Islamic religion gives us another example of serious cultural impositions. They give out the insane message that God wants young men and women to strap explosives to their bodies in a mission to destroy themselves along with untold numbers of random innocent bystanders. This religious madness is imposed upon brainwashed subjects and is a gross misuse of the power of religion. It not only overrides personal morality, but it erases the desire to live, to love, to procreate, and to survive. The enticement for such bizarre acts is that God loves martyrs and will reward them in heaven for serving the cause. For men, the reward is seventy-two vestal virgins. I'm not sure what the women bombers are promised, if anything. Similar madness was seen in World War II when Japanese Kamikaze Pilots crashed their airplanes into United States naval vessels. Japan has moved away from such nonsense, and it is only in dim retrospect that we view their history of violence as part of their duty bound honor to their Emperor Hirohito, who was also their God.

We must stand apart from religion's murderous policies and make every effort to encourage self-awareness in individuals so they might see themselves as unique and worthy of a good life. All religious *derangements* need to be rejected if we are to take full responsibility for our own lives. We do not need religions to dictate our moral lives. We are quite capable of making our own choices. Our lives are much too important than to allow ourselves to be tainted with the brush of religion's immoral hypocrisy.

Soul, Our Moral Compass

It is our soul that is our moral compass, and the bedrock of our valuing. This inner spiritual sense of self is the voice that integrates the perceptions of our intellect, emotion, imagination, and memory. Morality lies deep within the psyche of our DNA and the interactive fabric of our evolved collective cultural consciousness. When we want to know what is the right thing to do in any particular circumstance, if we ask our soul, we will get a moral answer. Our soul self will always tell us that the best path for us is to be kind, loving, and cooperative, and fortunately most of us know this from early childhood. We celebrate this level of consciousness as the birth of civilization.

Morality was not in the forefront of cultural consciousness in the times when kings and lords ruled over peasants and commoners; nor was it evident in the time of slavery. For the downtrodden and disenfranchised, liberation is found only when people will stand up for civility and participate in revolution to ensure human rights. We have seen this in many circumstances, such as the American and French Revolutions, and even our own Civil War, when the belief in the rightness of one's cause gives courage to those willing to fight for a cause that is right. These moral commitments have been groundbreaking events in social evolution. Morality is the glue that binds the fabric of civil societies in our ongoing struggle for peace with human rights and freedom.

The Personal Nature of Altruism

Even if I am altruistic, I will not always be altruistic. It depends on the circumstances and the players involved. Humans differentiate between the recipients of their altruism. It is always a choice, and one that is usually selected from well-thought-out considerations. The first recipients of our altruism will be those in the family bloodline, followed by others who are known and who have important connections to us. We are inclined to help those for whom we have the greatest compassion—our own people, our friends, and members of our tribe. These are people with whom we have rapport and for whom we have caring. We belong to the same team. These are the people who protect and support us, and we will reciprocate. No contracts need to be written. In the earliest of humans, there was loyalty to the tribe. We have been "our brother's keeper" for a very long time.

This drive toward benevolence is a genetic instinct that favors survival. More than survival—there is a force of energy within us that wants to thrive and to actualize our potential. And most of us know that it is up to us to make it happen, because God (the father) will not grant us favors and deny the next petitioner. The Force of a Natural God brings rain down on all of us without prejudice to our station, our nation, our race, or our faith. It is up to us to build and manage our own umbrellas and canoes.

Morality and Soul in Domestic Animals

There are plenty of signs of moral behavior among higher-level animals. We see this especially in our domesticated dogs and cats that treat us with affection and caring as well as loyalty. They sense early on that they are part of a family group. In the case of dogs, we also see that they have a fierce impulse to protect us. They would risk their own lives for their master. We might assume that this is some rudimentary moral sensing. It is more than just the "not biting of the hand that feeds us" mentality. Dogs want to belong as members of the pack within the family of man.

Dogs also find their place in the dominance hierarchy as they express deference to those they perceive as stronger. They will quickly turn belly-up on their backs to expose their vulnerable underside to any dog or human who they see as dominant. This is a clear body message that says, "Kill me if you must, but I will yield to you if you let me survive." Dogs are also capable of expressing shame. This is part of their sense of where they belong within the hierarchy of the pack. They sense the signals of disapproval and know which dogs are superior to them in the pack. When dogs are reprimanded for failing to meet a standard set by their human master, most will express shame! We have all witnessed a dog walking away with its tail between its legs. Imagine that! Here is a level of consciousness in an animal from the wild sensing that it is not living up to its master's expectations.

If I ask myself whether these animals have a soul, I would have to say that I believe they do, albeit somewhat limited in scope. They express affection, appreciation, gratitude, and a playful, joyous spirit in body language that is completely understood. Consider the tail wagging on the dog when they greet us or when they get praise. As for cats, consider how they purr when they are petted.

Situational Morality

Our own moral behavior will vary with particular circumstances. For example, none of us wants to be caught with his hand in the cookie jar, but if Mom is not around, one cookie might be okay. Similarly, If a teacher is watching, we won't look at our neighbor's paper during an exam, but if the coast is clear we might take a glance, even though we know we shouldn't. As adults, the stakes are higher. Many humans can be seduced to sell their souls for money or fame. Greed and perceived status are the basis of the temptations that cause us to lie, steal, cheat, and betray ourselves as well as others. Both beckon us to abandon our moral high ground. We rationalize our shortcomings by making excuses to convince ourselves that there is no real harm in what we have done. These lies attempt to relieve our guilt, but mostly they help us delude ourselves into believing that we won't get in trouble or be caught. We tell ourselves, "It's just for this one-time opportunity. I can live with the guilt. This transgression won't hurt anybody, and I deserve a break." And so on and so forth, we rationalize to let ourselves off the hook.

We lie to ourselves even though we know better. Consider the corporate corruption such as the not too distant Enron scandal, or the Ponzi scheme perpetrated by Bernie Madoff and his co-conspirators. Even the major banks (with support from a Congress that loosened their banking oversight regulations) gave way to the corrupt practice of encouraging subprime loans, and more recently illegal mortgage foreclosures without proper documentation. One would think that banks and our elected officials should be our most trusted institutions. But greed is extremely compelling and is the overriding consideration for the consequences that lead to corruption and the degradation of the moral fibers of society.

> *To educate a person in mind and not in morals is to educate a menace to society.*
> —Theodore Roosevelt

Roosevelt was absolutely right, which is why it is imperative that moral and ethical issues are dealt with early and continually in one's education. Morality must be a high value for all cultures on the planet if we are to build our utopian *Heaven on Earth*. In most societies, including our own, morality is not uniform. Some of us would never cause harm to others, while others would not think twice about harming others if the reward seemed worth it. We all fall on a continuum somewhere between that which is ideal and that which is repellent to most of us.

The following short list of behaviors demonstrates how we might differ on these polarities. You may want to *rate yourself to examine your current level of self-understanding* in this regard.

	5	4	3	2	1	
Honesty						Dishonesty
Forgivenes						Retribution
Kindness						Hostility
Caring						Indifference
Respect						Disrespect

Most of us will lean toward the moral side because we know in the long run that it pays off. We know from experience and observation that we will be treated well by others, we will be respected, we will have a positive reputation that will precede us, and that doors of opportunity will open for us as we contribute to building a society that is moral and just. We learn that if we behave morally, we will get social approval and others will have confidence in us. This works for us genetically because when we compete for a mate, we will be more likely to have success, and our DNA will get passed along to build this trait of strength in our progeny.

But there is something deeper in the human spirit that motivates humans in the give and take of relationships, and that something is kindness. Kindness is more than a stimulus and predictable response contract—it is about love. If our soul is touched by the kindness of another person, our natural urge is to want to reciprocate. We have a desire to live up to that kindness, to be deserving of it. Humans have a deep need to be loved and to belong.

Character and Morality

There can be no doubt that mutually beneficial and moral reciprocity in our relationships provides us with inner strength. We call this *character* and recognize it in others when we know and trust that their moral behavior is predictable and dependable. Character is fundamentally an expression of our inner spiritual life. It reveals the truth about our strengths or weakness and of how we will behave when the chips are down. If a person with the strong moral fiber of character inadvertently hurts another person by word or deed, she will immediately feel discomfort and know that she has done something that was not right. She will not feel "good" about it and she will not feel "good" about herself. Her inner voice of conscience will say, "I have betrayed my spirit, my inner sense of knowing what is right. I have acted against my own moral code."

This is why truth is so important. Truth resonates in harmony within our human spirit. If we lie, or cheat, or break a promise, we break the harmonic resonance within. We knock ourselves "off center." Morality keeps us aware that there are clear boundaries between telling the truth and lies. We know that it is better to be loving and considerate as opposed to being indifferent to the consequences our behavior may have on others.

The Synthesis of DNA and Experience

The wisdom that directs the instincts of mammals and other animals to feed and protect their babies is embedded in the genetic memory of our DNA. We find ourselves behaving this way automatically. This DNA endowment is enhanced by the assimilation of our moral learning with our life experiences. All that we have learned from experience are adaptations that become embedded in our DNA and are passed along to our progeny, and all ensuing generations. Most humans today, for example, have learned that it is important to be trusted and known to others as a dependable and worthwhile person. We have assimilated and synthesized this information in three ways: (1) through the genetics from our ancestral heritage, (2) by seeing that we have choices and choosing to behave in moral ways, and (3) from being aware of the outcomes from the choices we have made.

The learning of these moral choices is a subtle process and comes to us as we become able to accurately read the social cues of acceptance and rejection. These messages, delivered by body language, tone of voice, and direct comments, give us feedback from significant others and let us know if we are on track.

As our morality evolves and continues to assimilate what we have learned from experience, we gradually come to the awareness that we are truly here to serve each other. It is our moral behavior that makes everything work. Our families, our communities, and our employment are all supported and rooted in morality. In a very real sense, we are all trying to find our way as to how best to fit into this interactive community of service.

CHAPTER ELEVEN

Consciousness Is Our Spirituality

All the possibilities of your human destiny are asleep in your soul.
—John O'Donahue[48]

Consciousness is our awareness of our inner soul self within the context of our psychological and social lives. This would include, for example, our perception, cognition, memory, and morality, as well as the full range of our sensory and emotional networks. Consciousness is our voice within that tells us we have options, we have ideas, and we have free will. All these dimensions contribute to our sense of purpose, our determination of will, and whatever wisdom we may have assimilated in trying to find our best path. Consciousness opens a wider lens to the life of our spirit, including empathy, compassion, and our capacity to love. It is our highest sense of personal and social awareness in all our relationships. Consciousness is the force that drives our quest in life to realize our possibilities.

I think of consciousness as my soul. It is my soul that mediates and integrates my thoughts, choices, and actions while fine-tuning my stability and spiritual balance. My soul is the product of both my genetic endowment and what I have learned from experience. It is this integration of our biology with our mental states that guides us. To access this state we need to pause and behold our selves in the context of our lives. Consciousness is an evolutionary outcome, a miracle of our bio-spiritual synthesis.

---

[48] O'Donahue's, *Anam Cara*, 30.

Dwight Webb, PhD

The Rigidities of Faith

Faith, on the other hand, is a belief system that has no such bio-spiritual connection. Faith may be rooted in observable facts from our own experience or it may be attached to the myths, superstitions, and social traditions passed on to us by our culture, or both. For example, religions claim that the mystery of life may be understood by having faith, without relying on evidence, logic, or reasonable perceptions of reality. Faith has been a comforting choice for billions of people who want an answer to the mystery of life but do not want to raise questions about the details of missing evidence. Those of us less invested in faith with our religion avoid the angst of not having answers for everything by happily accepting the truth that life is a wonder-filled mystery, an amazing journey.

The rigidities of undocumented and unquestioned faith have delayed the evolution of our personal spiritual consciousness by shaping the norms of the culture to focus on myths and metaphors as absolute truths. There is no option for debate. This has led us away from seeing the truth that the Force of a Natural God is within all living things. This quest for heightened awareness is a continuing process of meeting the challenges of the barriers that are designed as obstacles to our seeking to actualize our potential.

Spiritual awareness is about integrating our present with significant experiences from our past, and our expectations and visions of our future. As we progress, we see that it is important not to focus our thoughts on past regrets or future fears, except as these guide us away from mistakes and danger. Such negative energy will only disrupt our ability to be fully present and blur our vision for our future. The truth of this was told eloquently more than eight centuries ago in the following piece from the classic book of philosophic poems *The Rubaiyat of Omar Khayyam:*

> *Ah! My Beloved, Come fill the Cup that clears*
> *Today of past Regrets and future Fears*
> *Tomorrow?—Why, Tomorrow, I may be*
> *Myself with Yesterday's Sev'n Thousand Years*[49]

---

[49] Omar Khayam, *Rubaiyat,* 5th ed. Poem number XXI (New York: Three Sirens Press: 1933).

To live in the now, with a positive attitude, is a major factor in contributing to our personal well-being and our ability to live our lives fully. By putting our energies into acts of love, respect, caring, forgiveness, encouragement, and acceptance, we enhance all of our relationships. These are but a few of the more obvious spiritual gifts we give to each other in the course of our daily lives. These gifts are the foundation of friendships, families, and communities. They are the spiritual connections from the core of who we are as people. It is how we know that we can trust each other, cooperate, and build our institutions and communities for the common good. These traditions in which we give of our spirit have been handed down from our earliest history and are the roots that have given us the strength to build nations with laws and the valuing of human rights.

Our consciousness today is largely determined by the enlightened quality of nurturing that we have received from our families, friends, and communities. Best selling author, Mitch Albom, reminds us, "The way you get meaning into your life is to devote yourself to loving others, devote yourself to creating something that gives you purpose and meaning."[50]

There is a palpable resonance when we are spiritually connected in our reciprocal relationships with others. Love promotes survival and life development, always favoring physical strength and beauty, as well as the spiritual strengths of intelligence and imagination. These are the adaptations that continue to move us forward. It is in remembering to be grateful for all the love in our lives that we begin to understand what is truly sacred.

Our Brother's Keeper

With all respect to this emphasis on love, we must not be in denial about the evil that resides in the ignorance and pathology of those who would randomly kill and subjugate others to their greedy purposes and distorted need for dominance. As our brother's keepers, we need to be more generous and compassionate with our resources as we face up to our responsibilities to the hungry, the ill, the homeless, the criminals, and

---

[50] Mitch Albom, *Tuesdays with Morrie: An Old Man, a Young Man on Life's Greatest Lessons* (New York: Wheeler Publications, 1999), 43.

all others who are too disabled by their present condition to be able to turn their present lives around. Those of us who are doing well know that we must provide help when it is needed for any passengers sharing our planet.

As stewards of the Earth, we are responsible for the quality of life for all things that sustain us—for the quality of our water and air, and for the multitude of resources from our good Mother Earth.

Our concern and compassion for others will surely emerge from the vitality of our inner spiritual life. We want opportunities for all to evolve toward wellness, honesty, justice, and respect as they meet challenges in their lives. It is our individual and collective effort in this regard that will lead us to moral action and to open doors for serving the greater good.

We are slowly moving away from greed, intolerance, and dishonesty toward a state of consciousness and vitality that provides us with the vision and strength to act with compassion in serving to enhance health for all life on the planet. There are no higher spiritual realms into which we may enter.

CHAPTER TWELVE

Tapping The Force Within

And that inverted Bowl we call The Sky,
Whereunder crawling coop't we live and die,
Lift not thy hands to It for help—for It
Rolls impotently on as Thou or I.
—Omar Khayyam[51]

Errors in Prayers

To whom are we praying? Why do we pray? What are our prayers about? Are we praying to a Father figure in the skies above us? Do we think He might reward us if we have been good or judge us and punish us if we behave badly? The answer to these last two questions is yes.

Growing up in the Western world, children's prayers are most often about asking God for special favors and making promises that their parents want them to make in order to shape behavior. This is the Santa Claus prayer syndrome, wherein we don't want to miss out on our personal allotment of goods and services because of our poor behavior. We leave the decisions of our fate in the hands of God. We believe that this God is omnipotent and omnipresent, aware of every feather that falls off a bird and every pleading prayer that falls from the lips of six billion people all at the same time.

When friends tell me that they are praying for someone who they believe is sick or in distress (maybe even me), I have trouble picturing a

---

[51] Omar Khayam, *Rubaiyat*, number LII.

God who would respond with, "Well, okay, you're a good person (one of my favorites). If you want it done, I'll do it! If you say they deserve saving, I'll put them on my savings list." The horror of this kind of God is that it suggests that if someone did not get remembered in prayer, then that person would just have to suffer or die. The delusional game we play when we pray in this superstitious way is called "covering our butts, and the butts of our family and friends, with our prayers."

When something good happens to us we believe our prayers have been answered, and when something bad happens, we hear the cliché, "God has a reason for everything." Just to be on the safe side, we excuse God for these omissions. These statements portray an outrageous view of a vindictive and whimsical God who rolls the dice to determine our fate.

Many of the prayers that I learned growing up were ones that most children memorized. They were most usually scheduled around meals, bedtimes, or services in church.

- Prayers of hymns, thanksgiving and gratitude for blessings bestowed
- Prayers asking God for forgiveness and/or personal protection
- Prayers of supplication, making a humble and earnest entreaty beseeching God to grant me special consideration

Looking at these, they might all seem reasonable. But leaving it to God in this way means never understanding our part in making these petitions happen. When these prayers don't get answered, we most often fail to see the connection with our own lack of effort in doing something for ourselves. We might be more inclined to think,

- God does not love me.
- I do not deserve to have my prayer answered, because I am not worthy.
- God is punishing me for something.

As a result of these erroneous conclusions, we learn to fear God. We continue to feel guilty and unworthy and we become suspicious and wonder what He is going to do if we should happen to displease Him by stepping out of line. If we are going to have a meaningful relationship with our God, we will have to take him out of this inverted bowl we call the sky.

Looking Within

They would have inner peace.
But will not look within.
—Joshua Liebman

Prayer is not about being one of six billion petitioners to the manager in the sky; it is about *tapping into our God-given inner strength of our spiritual wisdom*. Rabbi David Cooper writes, "The urge to call out to God is always answered simultaneous as it is spoken, for ultimately there is no difference between the caller and that to which it calls."[52]

The quote of Cooper's above seems to say it all . . . our questions *and* answers are within. Francis Vaughn writes, "God dwells within, and if we want to grow, to evolve and progress on a spiritual path, we must find the inner teacher; the spirit and truth that will guide us to wholeness and self-realization."[53] I think of my inner teacher as my soul.

We all yearn for direct connection and a meaningful relationship with what we think of as a Higher Power, and we all want to know how we are a part of it. But we have been largely unaware of who is in charge of our spiritual life and how we find meaning and purpose. We bring our humble wondering to face the great and magnificent mystery of this unknowable Higher Power, Creative Force, or God by any other name. Even with our inability to understand the mystery, does anyone really question that there is some inexplicable force in the universe? Isn't it also just as clear that we are *of* that force? If we recognize and accept this force as being within us, then surely we can tap into it.

The question is: how do we tap into our inner spirit and lay claim to our inner wisdom? It is within this core of our being that *we will find our prayers will only be answered with our own responses, our own choices and our own actions.*

---

[52]   Cooper, *God Is a Verb*.

[53]   Francis Vaughn, *The Inward Arc* (Berkeley: Shambala: 1986), 179.

[34]   Rober Wuthnow, *After Heaven* (Berkeley, University of Calfifornia Press: 1998), 198.

Prayer, Introspection, and Reflection

> *The point of spiritual practice is not to elevate*
> *An isolated set of activities over the rest of life*
> *But to electrify the spiritual impulse that animates all of life*
> Robert Wuthnow[34]

I think of prayer as entering into a sacred time within myself to engage the truth of my own soul as I seek and choose the best paths on my journey in life. This tapping into the source of my own inner strength is asking my soul self to show up for my own life and to hold myself accountable for what I deep down know will be in my best interest.

I am reaching inward to seek awareness of my soul self and realizing that I am capable of making positive choices. For example, I sometimes wake up in the morning a bit groggy, with a bit of a negative attitude about getting up and getting going. This morning, I paused and realized that I needed an attitude adjustment, and just realizing this made it happen. My mood shifted to the possibilities of the day.

I also find it helpful to set time aside throughout the day to reflect on my life, to wonder, to explore, and to consider my best options. To do this, it helps if I can make a time without interruptions and other distractions from the social and task-oriented contexts of my daily routines. I take time to reflect on my sense of who I am, and what it is I truly value.

Sometimes this spiritual reflection will come to me when I am on my tractor cutting a path in the hay fields. Sometimes I am blown away by my awareness of the beauty surrounding me. Often when I am touched by my inner spirit in this way, my eyes get moist as I acknowledge the many blessings in my life. These spiritual moments are key for me in creating a connection with nature and the Force of God I sense within me. In times like these I feel very grateful.

I suspect that most of us let our social life, our friendships, and our career choices play too dominant of a role in defining who we are. We want and need these friendships because they nurture us. But we are more than these definitions and activities, and we need to take time out to consider our wholeness of who we are to ourselves. We can do this without disrupting or losing our important friendships. Taking time for inner reflection and sorting out our priorities will enhance all the rest of our lives, including our relationships.

We need not keep these spiritual moments secret, nor should we make light of them as being too existential as we seek a deeper understanding of ourselves. To discount these times of reflection is to be flippant and disrespectful while disregarding our own spiritual development. While it is a good to have the warmth and lightness of spirit that having a sense of humor brings to us, it is imperative that we take ourselves seriously in our quest for actualization. The outcome will be to come face to face with our awareness and connection to the Natural Force of God within us.

In Lieu of an Institutional God

As we come to accept our inner God in lieu of our Institutional God, there need be no loss of belief in the Creator, the Supreme Force, or the Higher Power regardless of the name we give to the mystery. Rather, we may celebrate that we can sense that the Force of this mystery is coursing through our veins in every moment.

I choose to go about my day with feelings of gratitude, and find that it makes me feel a sense of humility and of connectedness with my larger world. Gratitude is my most prayerful attitude.

Our greatest freedom is to choose our attitude about any given set of circumstances.
—Victor Frankl[54]

---

[54] Victor Frankl, *Man's Search for Meaning* (New York: Washington Square Press, 1963).

Attitude Is Everything

Professor William R. Parker was my most important mentor.[55] On one occasion he suggested to me that prayer is an attitude. I puzzled about this for some years before I came to see that our attitudes are implicitly and inextricably invested with our beliefs, our values, and our choices. For example: if I want to become more dependable, respectful, and trustworthy in my relationships, I must project attitudes and actions that are more dependable, respectful, and trustworthy. I have to answer my own prayers. Attitudes followed by action go hand in glove. These are our practical everyday choices based in a belief that this is a desirable way of being and it is *up to us* to manifest them if they are going to get done.

Another way attitude is important in my spiritual quest is that I can choose to enter into prayer, reflection, or soul conversation with hope and optimism, as opposed to doubt and cynicism. It is my choice to invite these positive attitudes into my consciousness in everything I do. I choose to be open to experience and to possibilities. I choose to have an attitude that believes in the goodness of the world, and I choose an attitude of remaining hopeful and optimistic. It is my intention and belief that my life will be enhanced if I make these choices consciously. These optimistic attitudes are based in a belief that there is an innate force of goodness in my life, a natural inclination to put my best foot forward. It is in the holding of positive attitudes that I find the expression of love and caring for the well being of others. In addition to holding positive attitudes, I must be willing to act on them. Acts of love are the spiritually tangible manifestations of our soul, our interface with the Force of God within.

---

[55] William R, "Cherry" Parker was my most significant mentor in both my undergraduate and graduate programs at the University of Redlands. I am extremely grateful to him for modeling, supporting, and encouraging my positive outlook on life.

Beliefs

Beliefs are extremely important in our lives. If we don't believe something, we tend to close our mind to it and set it aside. But if we are open to consider that here might be something that is worthwhile, we then can consider moving forward to check it out. We just might come to believe in something we did not think was possible. It's a matter of greeting life with openness. The first step of seeking strength and clarity is to *believe* that we already have strength and clarity within. If we have doubts, we must explore from whence these doubts came and work toward the release of their hold on us.

When we believe that we have this inner force, we begin to understand that we have the power to shape our lives. This belief activates the vitality of our spirit as we see that we have the capacity to become what we believe is possible. We come to understand that this aliveness of our spirit is our most important human dimension because it directs all others. While common sense tells us that our spirituality is more complex and multidimensional than simply cognitive, emotional, and physical, many people are still not comfortable in claiming their spirituality. The priority of our culture has been to emphasize our logic and rationality. This has made it very convenient to leave spiritual matters to religion.

We are ready to leave these rigid rational routines and consider the truth of our ignorance and the folly of neglecting to understand or attend to our spiritual life. Our lives are not created for leaving the meaning of things unexamined. To the contrary, it is our nature to examine everything. On our spiritual journey, we are meant to love, to be with family and friends, to enjoy good health with strong bodies and clear minds, and to hunger for engagement and meaning in life. We are meant to be whatever we are capable of becoming.

If you can imagine your possibilities, you can become your possibilities. Attitudes set the framework for the foundation of beliefs. To integrate these possibilities into our lives, we need to open our attitudes and to believe these ways of being are within our reach. Gandhi helped us to see the importance of this kind of envisioning when he said, "We must *be* the change we wish to see in the world."[56]

---

[56] Readers may refer to www.mohatmagandhi for quotations.

Choices, Commitment, and Actions

The integration of these essential personal dimensions will provide the elements for the lens through which we experience our inner spiritual life. Our attitudes must be open, our beliefs founded on our sincere efforts to connect with the force of God within, and our choices carefully measured with our commitment to thoughtfully act upon our decisions.

It is important to have an attitude of friendly compassion as you ask questions of your soul self, such as,

- What do I really want?
- Am I willing to take the courage to become my best self?
- Do I believe in my potential?
- Do I have an optimistic attitude, and if not, why not?
- Can I open myself experience the humility and gratitude for the magnificent mystery of life?
- Finally, am I willing to cooperate with the natural movement of my life toward health and well-being?

Are these not essentially prayers? They are questions we are asking our soul selves about how we conduct our lives, what we value, and how we come to our beliefs and make our choices. The problem with religious prayers is that most people expect an outside God to fix things, when in fact it is really up to us to take care of ourselves.

Check in with your soul with your questions. It will help you recognize any negative energy that is keeping you passive and/or stuck, and help you to mobilize your positive attitudes and spirits. I find that if I continue to do this and remain willing to wait for answers, my soul will be a dependable consultant in these matters.

Do you have the patience to wait
Till your mud settles and the water is clear?
Can you remain unmoving
Till the right action arises by itself?
—Tao Te Ching[57]

---

[57] The *Tao Te Ching* is a book written in ancient China by Lao Tzu, the keeper of the Imperial Library, who was well known for his wisdom. It is one of the

The Fullness of Our Spirit

If anything is ubiquitous in our lives, it is our spirit. Every conscious act and thought of ours tells us something about our spirit. These actions and thoughts arise from our inner self, which guides our attitudes, our values, our beliefs, and our choices. It is our spirit that ignites and drives our vitality, our passion to live life fully. In very tangible and practical ways, our spirituality is the essence of who we are. I very much like the way Roberto Assagioli expressed this idea so directly: "Spiritual refers not only to experiences traditionally considered to be religious, but to all the states of awareness, all the human functions and activities."[58]

Given that our spirit fuels our vitality, isn't it odd that we have neglected to claim, develop, and honor this dimensions that relates so directly to the quality of our lives? We have been largely unaware of who or what is in charge of our spiritual life. We need to understand that it is our spirit that drives the choices in our lives, and that we will become what we make of ourselves.

We are beginning to realize that we do not need religious institutions, with all their intermediaries and hierarchical bureaucratic frameworks, in order to experience the Natural force of God. Why would any God want to be defined by any institution or have that institution select and certify certain humans to intervene on our behalf while others are ignored?

When your soul awakens, your destiny becomes urgent with creativity
—John O'Donohue[59]

Consciousness is our spiritual adaptation endowed by evolution and embedded in our DNA. And we must be open to seeking our destiny if we are to fully develop. Many people are not open to this idea, and for them life may be one of routine plodding. Our attitude must be one of openness to discovery if we are to integrate what we have learned from our experiences with our sense of self and our potential. It is this ongoing

---

most influential books in history. www.taoteching.com.

[58] Robert Assagioli, *Psychosynthesis: A Manual of Principles and Techniques* (New York: Viking Penguin, 1973).

[59] O'Donahue, *Anam Cara*, 111.

synthesis that makes up the core of our being, our soul self. Prayerful reflection and meditation are the search engines available for developing our wholeness.

It is our soul that is our spiritual center. It is the awareness of our self as an autonomous being in the vastness of the universe. Seeking our spiritual development is about being fully human and it is our soul that is concerned with truth, justice, and love and the accompanying respect, caring, and compassion that we are capable of in all our relationships. Carolyn Myss reminds us: "We are meant to move toward self-discovery and spiritual maturity, to be ready and able to live a life that matters to us and those around us."[60]

It is our spirit that is the hard drive guiding our ability to express love in our relationships. We don't typically talk or think about how it is that these spiritual acts of ours arise from our soul within, but if we pause and think about it for even a brief moment, we see that we are responsible for developing these personal qualities of awareness for ourselves.

As humans, we are much more complex than just our intellect, our emotions, or our physical beings. It is in our DNA infrastructure to have hope, gratitude, and reverence, among a thousand other spiritual nuances in all our relationships as we negotiate and navigate our daily lives. Our spiritual life is driven by all of these. Although there are plenty of rational and logical reasons that could explain much of our behavior, they do not do justice to the depth of spirit present in a great friendship or a beautiful love relationship. *It is interesting to note that we express all of our spiritual acts quite naturally and spontaneously without being attached to any religion.*

Most of us believe that good things can be made to come to pass and that we may be helpers in this process, especially if we believe that our hard work and good decisions will make a difference. These spiritual actions arising from our soul carry the message, "Do the right thing, and leave this planet a little better than you found it."

---

[60]   Carolyn Myss, *Anatomy of the Spirit* (New York: Three Rivers Press: 1997), 290.

Prayer as Intention and Action

If there is a recipient of our prayers that would be our soul, our best self, the potential we have for becoming. While we can clearly see the force of a Natural God all around us, the only God we can truly know is the force of God within. My soul tells me the truth and tells me to tell the truth. It also tells me to be kind to others. Having a conversation with my soul is entering into a sacred moment within myself, trying to engage the truth of my own life. For me, the best place (but not the only place) for this silent and inner connecting conversation is in nature, the woods, the seas, a river, desert, lake, or field—any of these will provide the quiet wonder that will set the stage for opening to that which I see as sacred within us.

These prayerful moments are about being open to the awareness that the inner wisdom of my soul will not desert me or deceive me in any way. It is the source of my potential to become my best self, and it is up to me if I am to actualize this potential.

Most of us, including myself, don't find this easy, and we fall short in various ways and degrees. Prayer is our intention, but it must be more than that; it must be *our commitment to action* that supports this intention that moves us toward growth. The connection we have with our own soul opens to us on our spiritual journey. There is, within each of us, a resource of potential for such growth. It is good to remember that the word *inspired* literally means living in the spirit. Allow yourself to be inspired!

In addition to retreating to nature, prayer is also an ongoing process in our every waking moment as we choose our attitudes and behaviors. For example, consider that our attitudes, underlying kindness, caring, forgiveness, and respect are all motivated by our inner spirit. They are the outcome of our soul searching and soul choosing. Part of prayer is choosing what we want to become and how we want to be in our life. Like anything we choose, the foundational attitudes will require our commitment, effort, and discipline if we are to shape our lives to our best interest and to the common good. My soul force is my natural inclination to put my best foot forward without a second thought. Intention is our prayer and that prayer is answered with our action.

Unloading Our Burdens

If someone has offended you and you are feeling angry, disappointed, put down, rejected, humiliated, or just plain misunderstood, underappreciated, and judged, you need to look at those wounds and check in with your soul to see from whence this residual anger, bitterness, or resentment arises. Understanding this, and releasing the burden of this toxic energy through an honest appraisal of the situation, will move you in the direction of forgiveness.

We need to let go of our burdens. We need to forgive ourselves as well as others. As long as we carry the burdens of anger guilt and hostility, we will not be free. These are the demons that will haunt us with self-doubt and continue to present obstacles and excuses, for us to remain victims, when what we really want is to move forward. We need to forgive and to let go without shame. To let go of toxic soul burdens is to make room to let love into our lives. Forgiveness starts with understanding that the behavior of any offending person is his or hers to own, as he or she makes his or her way along his or her own path of existence. We have the choice of forgiving these people for their shortcomings, since we are all working to find our own way.

We are all endowed with the capability of connecting with our consciousness and discovering the truth about our own strengths and shortcomings. Tapping into our spirit is tapping into our soul, our vitality, and our love of life. This is the path that will accelerate the continuing of our most important work in progress, the building of *Heaven on Earth*.

I close with the following poem by Siegried Sassoon.

Credo

The heaven for which I wait has neither guard nor gate.
The God in whom I trust shall raise me not from dust.
I shall not see that heaven for which my days have striven,
Nor kneel before the God toward whom my feet have trod.

But when from this half-human evolvement man and woman
Emerge, through brutish Me, made strong and fair and free,
The dumb forgotten dead will be the ground they tread
And in their eyes will shine my deathless hope divine.[61]

---

[61] This poem by Siegried Sassoon is from the *Harvard Educational Review* 18, no. 3 (summer 1948).

Suggested Readings

Cooper, David. *God Is a Verb: Kabbalah and the Practice of Mystical Judaism.* New York: Riverbend Books, 1997.

Dawkins, Richard. *God the Delusion.* New York: Mariner Books, 2006.

Dawkins, Richard. Out of Eden: *A Darwinian View of Life.* New York: Basic Books, 1995.

Dennett, Daniel. *Darwin's Dangerous Idea: Evolution and the Meaning of Life.* New York: Simon and Schuster, 1995.

Dennett, Daniel. *Consciousness Explained.* Boston: Back Bay Books, 1992.

Dennett, Daniel. *Breaking the Spell.* New York: Penguin Group, 2006.

Harris, Sam. *The End of Faith.* New York: W. W. Norton and Co., 2006.

Harris, Sam. *Letter to a Christian Nation.* New York: Vintage Press, 2006.

Hitchens, Christopher. *God Is not Great: How Religion Poisons Everything.* New York: Mariner Books, 2007.

Kaufmann, Stuart. *Reinventing the Sacred: A New View of Science, Reason and Religion.* New York: Basic Books, 2008.

Khayyam, Omar. *The Rubaiyat of Omar Khayyam.* New York: Three Sirens Press, 1933.

Maslow, Abraham. *Toward the Further Reaches of Human Nature.* New York: Penguin Books, 1971.

Myss, Caroline, *Anatomy of the Spirit: The Seven Stages of Prayer and Healing.* New York: Three Rivers Press, 1997.

O'Donohue, John. *Anam Cara: Spiritual Wisdom from the Celtic World.* New York: Bantam Books. 1997.

Schmidt, Leigh Eric. *Restless Souls: The Making of American Spirituality.* San Francisco: Harper, 2005.

Valliant, George. *Spiritual Evolution: A Scientific Defense of Faith.* New York: Broadway Books, 2008.

Webb, Dwight. *The Soul of Counseling*. Atascadero: Impact Publishing, 2005.

Williamson, Marianne. *Everyday Grace*. New York: Riverhead Books, 2002.

Wuthnow, Robert. *After Heaven: Spirituality in America since the 1950s*. Berkeley: University of California Press. 1998.

Related Readings

Albanese, D. L. *Nature Religion in America: From the Algonquin Indians to the New Age.* Chicago: University of Chicago Press, 1991.

Alexander, R. D., and D. Tinkle, eds. *Natural Selection and Social Behavior.* New York: Chiron Press, 1981.

Allman, J. M. *Evolving Brains.* New York: Scientific American Library, 1999.

Anderson, R. F. *"Geomancy,"* in *The Power of Place: Sacred Ground in Natural and Human Environments,* edited by James A. Swan. Wheaton: Quest Books, 1991.

Appleyard, B., *Understanding the Present: Science and the Soul of Modern Man,* New York: Doubleday, 1992.

Atkins, P. *Creation Revised.* Oxford: W. H. Freeman, 1992.

Attenborough, David. *Quest in Paradise.* London: Luggerworth, 1960.

Barker, D. *Losing Faith in Faith.* Madison: Freedom from Religion Foundation Press, 1992.

Becker, E. *The Denial of Death.* New York: Free Press, 1973.

Beit-Hallahmi and Argyle. *The Psychology of Religious Behaviour: Belief and Experience.* London: Routledge, 1997.

Bellah, Robert. *Religion in Human Evolution.* Cambridge: Harvard University Press, 2011.

Berhony, K., *Ordinary Grace: An Examination of the Roots of Compassion, Altruism, and Empathy and the Ordinary Individuals Who Help Others in Extraordinary Ways,* New York: Riverhead Books, 1999.

Berlinerblau, J., *The Secular Bible: Why Nonbelievers Must Take Religion Seriously.* Cambridge: Cambridge University Press, 2000.

Campbell, J. *The Transformation of Myth through Time.* New York: Harper Perennial, 1990.

Eckhart, Meister. *The Soul is One with God.* New York: Macmillen, 1967.

Freeman, C. *The Closing of the Western Mind*. London: Heinemann, 2002.

Gawain. Shakti. *Living in the Light*. Mill Valley: Whatever Publishing, 1986.

Goodenough, Ursula. *The Sacred Depth of Nature*. Oxford: Oxford University Press, 2000.

Hamer, Dean. *The God Gene: How Faith Is Hardwired into the Genes*. New York: Doubleday, 2004.

Hauser, M. *Moral Minds: How Nature Designed Our Universal Sense of Right and Wrong*, New York: Ecco, 2006.

Hinde, R. A., *Why God Is Good: The Sources of Morality*. London:

Jacoby, S. *Freethinkers: A History of American Secularism*. New York: Holt, 2004.

Jammer, M. *Einstein and Religion*. Princeton: Princeton University Press, 2002.

Jung, Carl. *Modern Man in Search of a Soul*. New York: Brace and World-Harvest, 1933.

Kaufman, Walter. *The Faith of a Heretic*. Garden City: Doubleday & Co., 1961.

Kennedy, L. *All in the Mind: A Farewell to God*. London: Hodder and Stoughton, 1999.

Kornfield, J. *A Path with Heart: A Guide through the Perils and Promises of Spiritual Life*, New York: Bantam Books, 1993.

Kurtz P., ed. *Science and Religion: Are They Compatible?* Amherst: Prometheus, 2004.

Luc, Jean Marion. *God without Being*. Chicago: University of Chicago Press, 1991.

Maslow, Abraham. *Toward a Psychology of Being*, New York: Harper and Row, 1968.

Newberg, Andrew, and Mark Waldman. *How God Changes Your Brain*. New York: Random House, Ballantine, 2009.

Oliver, Mary. *New and Selected Poems*. Boston: Beacon Press, 1992.

Plimer, I. *Telling Lies for God: Reason vs. Creationism*. Milsons Point: NSW, 1994.

Rogers, Carl. *A Way of Being*. Boston: Houghton-Mifflin, 1980.

Sardello, Robert. *Love and the Soul*. New York: Harper Collins, 1995.

Shermer, M. *Why People Believe Weird Things: Pseudoscience, Superstition, and Other Confusions of Our Time*. New York: W. H. Freeman, 1997.

Shermer, M. *The Science of Good and Evil: Why People Cheat, Gossip, Care, Share, and Follow the Golden Rule*. New York: Holt, 2006.

Shermer, M. *How We Believe: The Search for God in an Age of Science*. New York: W. H. Freeman, 1999.

Silby, Uma. *Enlightenment on the Run: Everyday Life as a Spiritual Path*. San Rafael: Airo Press, 1993.

Sober, E., and D. S. Wilson. *Unto Others: The Evolution and Psychology of Unselfish Behavior*. Cambridge: Harvard University Press, 1998.

Stannard, R. *Doing Away with God? Creation and the Big Bang*. London: Pickering, 2003.

Swinburne, R. *The Existence of God*. Oxford: Oxford University Press, 2004.

Swan, James. *Nature as Teacher and Healer*. New York: Villard Books, 1992.

Tiger, L. *Optimism: The Biology of Hope*. New York, Anchor, 1979.

Vaughan, Francis. *Awakening Intuition*. New York: Anchor, 1979.

Watts, Alan. *The Sprit of Zen: A Way of Life*. New York: Grove Press, 1969.

Wolpert, L. *Six Impossible Things Before Breakfast: The Evolutionary Origins of Belief*. London: Faber and Faber, 2006.

Acknowledgements

Since this book is about my ideas, beliefs, and experiences, I am grateful to all the contributors who have significantly impacted and shaped my life. I have to start with my mother and father for the gift of the latest edition of my ancestral pool. They, along with my brother, provided the foundational family for my spiritual and spirited development. Their love, and encouragement is the source that shaped my human spirit, my compassion, my joy in life, and ultimately my motivation to write this book. Compassion is what this book is all about. This is the spiritual glue that keeps us connected and working for the common good as we build heaven on Earth.

My life has also been shaped by many friends, mentors, colleagues and students, who have shared their compassionate spirits with me over the years, engaging me in serious conversation as well as in more lighthearted times of laughter and joy. To be validated by kindred spirits is among the most meaningful and life-enhancing experiences any person can have. I want to mention a few people in particular who have helped me build the journey of my life in ways that have contributed to this book.

Foremost, I must acknowledge my mentor Cherry Parker, who was incredibly important to me in my college years as he lived his vision of life, with compassion. These along with his warmth and his great sense of humor, have been lifetime gifts for which I am forever grateful

I am also very thankful to my wife, Leslie, who joined me in bringing our daughter, Julia, home from Russia to create our family, adding immense value and meaning to my life. I appreciate my son Michael for a thoughtful read and helpful suggestions on my manuscript, and my son John for giving me his honest opinion concerning my earlier title for this book and then helping me brainstorm and create a current one. Thanks also for my sons David and Chris and my niece Lorrie Webb Grillo for their encouragement on this journey.

Thanks to friends who have given me their thoughts on my ideas and on my writing. Among these are: Karen Hailson Bouvier, Farley Andresen, Will Williams and Richard Merlin Riedman, all gentle souls who helped shape my message.

To Greg Goodman, Paul Treacy, Bert Whetstone, Jason Holder, Victor Messier, David Van Nuys, Heiko Haase, and Abel DeVries, my "soul brothers" and closest men friends, who have encouraged me and supported me from the beginning of my friendship with them. And to Ben Fowler who although we disagreed on how we viewed the human spirit, gave me critique that pushed me to work harder to explain myself.

I give special thanks to my daughter-in-law Tammi Webb for responding so quickly and creatively to my request for painting the pastoral piece on my book cover. I asked her to paint a bit of Heaven on Earth that would also show evidence of human hands on the farm, and she selected a sweet slice of paradise that is just outside the window of my office at home. It was just the right touch. Huge appreciation also to Scott Vigneault for color blending and typeface design for the cover.

I hold a very special appreciation for my friend and colleague Liam McCarthy, the founder of the Personal Counseling Institute in Dublin, Ireland. In teaching and planning with him for eight summers, he gave me the gift of opportunities and freedom to explore my ideas about spirituality as they interface with the counseling process. Although he passed away two years ago, his spirit remains very much with me. His generous encouragement was a gift of enormous proportion in contributing to the birthing of this book.

Several years ago, my friend and colleague Angelo Boy said, in an off-handed comment, "everyone has three books in them." Little did he know that this would cause me to say to myself, "Well I guess that means me, and I had better get busy." This being my third book, the pressure is off now, but I always appreciated that remark of his, as it unexpectedly awakened my own writing ambitions. And in this context, I thank the University of New Hampshire for supporting me in my writing by granting me six sabbatical leaves during my forty-two years as a professor in the Graduate Program in Counseling.

Gay Hendricks, a former student of mine, invited me to spend five summers teaching at the University of Colorado, in Colorado Springs. He, along with his colleague Barry Weinhold, had coauthored an important book on Transpersonal Counseling, and both provided a supportive period of growth for me in connecting with the foundations of secular spirituality.

And finally, to Phyllis Ross, a longtime friend, whose dedicated commitment to her Catholic faith inspired me to dig deeper into how best I might represent my opposing points of view. Her steadfast, irrational, and stubborn argument in support of her faith was inspirational, and her openness to bear with my criticisms kept our dialogue fresh, untainted, and frustrating, ultimately compelling me to clarify and articulate *what I have faith in and what I believe*. I hope I have been able to communicate this in my book.

Dwight Webb
Lee, New Hampshire
March, 2012

16384239R00076

Made in the USA
Lexington, KY
20 July 2012